DESTRUCTION OF LIFE

BY

SNAKES, HYDROPHOBIA,

ETC.

IN WESTERN INDIA

DESTRUCTION OF LIFE
BY
SNAKES, HYDROPHOBIA,
ETC.
IN WESTERN INDIA

ANONYMOUS

GYAN

Published by

Gyan Publishing House
5, Ansari Road
Daryaganj, New Delhi-110002
Phone: 011-47034999, 9811692060
E-mail: books@gyanbooks.com

Distribution Network
gyanbooks.com
India, USA, Canada, UK, Australia

ISBN: 978-93-6433-220-0 (HB)

First Published, 1880

2nd Impression 2024

Printed at: Gyan Press, Delhi.

DESTRUCTION OF LIFE BY SNAKES, HYDROPHOBIA, ETC. IN WESTERN INDIA
Author: ANONYMOUS

DESTRUCTION OF LIFE

BY

SNAKES, HYDROPHOBIA, ETC.

DESTRUCTION OF LIFE

BY

SNAKES, HYDROPHOBIA,

ETC.

IN WESTERN INDIA.

BY AN EX-COMMISSIONER.

Nunquam nimis dicitur
Quodnumquam satis dicitur.

LONDON:
W. H. ALLEN AND CO.
13 WATERLOO PLACE, S.W.
PUBLISHERS TO THE INDIA OFFICE.

1880.

the mortality from hydrophobia at an earlier date.

Made up, in a measure, of old detached memoranda, unmethodical arrangement will be noticed in these chapters: it is admitted, and must be excused, not only on the ground that if not in this imperfect form it probably would never have been put forward at all; and further, though some parts may fail to interest the general reader, and though not always in consecutive order, some particulars will be found *here* which have not been noticed by others. Proof from record and the highest authorities will be found quoted in support of some statements of a very startling character: for example, in regard to the extraordinary inequality in the geographical distribution and consequent irregularity in the mortality of districts, take one district of Bombay, Sholapoor—mortality in 1877, 4; Tanjore, a district of Madras, in the same year, 700.

There is the official record in support of the fact.

A satisfactory explanation can only be sup-

PREFACE.

The destruction of life in India from snakes and other preventible causes is now in an increased degree engaging attention in England, but there are some important facts which are not generally known, and some mischievous theories which ought to be rebutted.

There is also a very general impression that the subject has only recently engaged the attention of the authorities in India, but it will be shown that measures calculated to reduce the mortality from snakes were commenced twenty-four years ago. Attention was directed to plied by local authority on such points as these:—

Soil and climate as affecting snakes.

The average mortality from snake-bites.

The highest mortality.

The lowest.

Under what system was the lowest mortality arrived at?

During the period when rewards were withdrawn, was any other system for the destruction of snakes instituted?

Remedies and recoveries.

It should also be noted that the high rate of mortality in the Tanjore district is quite exceptional. Only a fraction of that mortality is found in Gangam or Kurnool.

Why Western India? Why not not call it the Bombay Presidency? One reason is, because it refers to other districts which are not, or were not, included in the Presidency:—

Upper Sind.

Hyderabad.

Kurachce.

Thur.

Nugger Parker.

Puneh Mahal.

These formerly were not included in the returns.

Sind can hardly now be ealled part of the Presidency.

Canara.—At the period referred to, this distriet belonged to Madras.

The seeond reason is, because the *Echis carinata*, to whieh many referenees will be found as the ehief agent of destruetion, extends a long way beyond the limits of the Bombay Presideney, from the Punjaub to Malabar, and further.

The term Western India is appropriate as in some sort conneeted with the geographical distribution of this deadly snake, whieh does not exist in Bengal, and is referred to by writers at Madras as insignifieant, though Dr. Russell, 1796, knew better, residing at Vizagapatam*: he never saw a live specimen, but

* As stated elsewhere, this reptile disappears at Vizagapatam, and is not found again till near Delhi.

he rightly identified the snake as Veryen pam, the Tamil name for *Echis carinata*.

It should also be noticed that in the Returns of recent years, the great increase of mortality is mainly owing to the addition of these seven districts, which were not included in the former period of 1856–59.

INTRODUCTION.

Attention in England, especially during the last year or two, has been awakened to the subject of the destruction of life from snake-bites, hydrophobia, &c., in India. There have been articles in thc papers, and an eminent Professor has given a lecture, of which, having only secn a very brief notice in thc "Times" of the 2nd of Dccember last, we will only remark that the Professor, lamenting the loss of human life, does not qucstion the substantial accuracy of the returns of mortality. It is satisfactory to note that this element of useless and vexatious discussion is eliminated by so great an authority. Allowing any amount of latitude to freedom of opinion, no man has a right to put forward his own *fanciful conjectures as proved facts,* or to stand forward as a champion of a do-nothing policy and preach a doctrine, unsupported by evidence, which, if adopted, would paralyse all effort. This is here referred to *in limine,* because such rash and unwarrantable assertions (*vide* Appendix D.), unless directly and emphatically contradicted, are calculated still further to confuse and complicate this already difficult subject.

Neither the magistrates nor any other authorities in India have ever stated that the returns are precisely correct. Allowing for cases which have escaped registration, the returns are substantially true: only a very small margin need be allowed for inaccuracies.

It should be noticed also, that these returns refer only to the districts under our Government: the whole mortality for all India would include the native states under Scindia, Holkar, &c., and also vast tracts of country like Gondwana.

The sensational dogma about fictitious snake-bites will be found more particularly noticed; it is unsupported by evidence.

The people of England can hardly entertain so low an opinion of the Magistrates and Police officers of India, as to suppose their vigilance is so feeble and so restricted. That they are cognizant of the fact that Datura poisoning is practised extensively, and especially on travellers on the great trunk roads. (This was brought under the notice of the Bombay Government so long ago as 1858 by Major Hervey.)

That three-fourths of all the inmates of the several lunatic asylums throughout India have themselves produced their disorder by bang and other preparations of *Cannabis sativa* or *Indica*.

They know also that Colonel Phayre is not the first official who has been poisoned for doing his duty, thereby making himself *ingrata persona*.

They, the Magistrates and Police, know all this and a great deal more; and yet according to the fictitious snake-bite dogmatists, thousands of lives are lost annually, and *the Magistrates and the Police know nothing about it!* The public will consider and judge whether it is possible that such crimes could be practised extensively without attracting the attention of the Police and the Magistrates. Officers of long and varied experience in the several districts of the Presidency have never heard of or met with such cases.

Without attempting to suggest what ought or might be done in Bengal or the other Presidencies, there is an efficient and sufficient machinery at hand in the Western Presidency, which may be worked to a satisfactory result; and within the average expenditure of the last twenty years. There are Wudders and other willing and efficient agents.

There are municipalities which can be taught to follow the example of Bangalore. There is a well-trained Police.

There is one serious want, that is, *there is no head.*

If one may presume to offer the suggestion —let one of the three Commissioners now performing the joint functions of Revenue and Police be appointed to the charge of the Police alone for the whole presidency. Abolish "Trilinguæ," let the three single gentlemen be rolled into one, as to the functions of Police. He requires no special qualifications except energy of mind and body, and no knowledge except what he can find in the Police and Magistcrial Records. The whole working of the system should rest with the Head of the Police, and the less *prominence given to this particular part of his duties the better.*

There are some points in the text of such importance, as to require prominent notice.

Referring to pages 62–63 on the subject of the enormous destruction of snakes at Rutnagerry in 1856–58. The fact (supported as it is by trustworthy evidence) must be considered of immense importance as proving (in defiance of those who advocate the do-nothing policy) what can be accomplished by strenuous and well-directed effort.

Its importance would have been recognised if this had been a single instance, perhaps with some mistrust,* but most fortunately similar operations, with like results, were carried out in the same district, by different agents, at intervals of several years.

Snakes, 115,921 were killed in 1872.
„ 140,828 „ in 1876.

As affecting the mortality of the district, it appears the deaths from snake-bites were—

	Deaths.
1856 . . .	257
1857 . . .	65

The worst year since 1856 :—

1875 . . .	144

In 1876, 140,828 snakes were killed, and in 1877 the mortality was reduced to 30, the lowest attained since operations commenced in 1856.

Punjab in 1875, 144,542 snakes were killed, but the Punjab means many districts. Rutnagerry is one district.

* As to the possibility of such enormous destruction.

DESTRUCTION OF LIFE

BY

SNAKES, HYDROPHOBIA, ETC.

CHAPTER I.

BEFORE entering on a comparison of returns and other details, we advisedly give prominence to, and beg the particular notice of the reader to, this chapter, which regards a theory extensively promulgated to the effect that *no reduction in the mortality is feasible.*

On this point we at once join issue, and declare distinctly that it is a grave and mischievous error, mischievous and dangerous in the highest degree, beeause it is ealeulated to paralyse all effort; in point of fact it has already done so, in the Madras Presideney, where no rewards are offered.

Whether there is any justifieation or support to the above theory, or whether it is not absolutely disproved, will now appear.

It involves a repetition, but the particular facts are not (elsewhere in the text) as prominently set forth as their great importance deserves.

There is no reason to suppose that snakes were not formerly as numerous in Bombay as in other parts of the Conean at the present time. We infer from what Dr. Ives, Surgeon on board the flag-ship, wrote,—1776—that there were many poisonous snakes. He enumerates several, but identification, exeept of the eobra, is diffieult.

To eompare a period with returns to a remote period when there were none, would be unsatisfaetory.

Dr. Ives' evidence is good and trustworthy, judging by the aeeuracy of his narrative of other events, for example, regarding the pirate ehief Angria, or the eapture of Viziadroog, but we only require his evidence up to a certain point, viz. as to the *probable* amount of mortality long ago, and that the same number of snakes existed in Bombay as in the neighbouring islands.

The particular fact now submitted does not rest on the testimony of any one witness, but *on the records of the hospital* at Bombay, and is referred to by Dr. Morehead.

This is the fact—there were in Bombay only fourteen deaths from snake-bites in five years, population (1856) 500,000—a fraction below THREE DEATHS A YEAR.

In 1856, at Rutnagherry, population 665,238, there were 257 deaths in that year.

Then a great effort was made, and the mortality in the next year was reduced to 65. For further particulars in succeeding years, *vide* page 20 and elsewhere.

The mortality rose again, but never to half the standard of 1856, and the last annual return gives a mortality of 30, or 227 *less than in* 1856.

The reader will judge for himself whether it is not here distinctly proved that the mortality from snakes is susceptible of reduction.

Another proof is to be found on the Bombay records. The mortality in the twelve districts of the Presidency and province of Sattarah was—

In 1856	. . .	575
1857	. . .	446
1858	. . .	368

Difference between the first and the third year, 207.

Another proof that the mortality can be and has been reduced.

There will be found repetition in this brief memorandum, not vain or purposeless, but insistance on important points about which there is existing controversy.

The clergyman in his pulpit, or the barrister in court for his client, insist upon and repeat, *iterum iterumque,* the same arguments or chain of reasoning; so now some important points will be reverted to again and again.

The life of one man depends on the sagacity and perhaps insistance of his counsel; the lives of many thousands depend on a right judgment of this momentous question.

Many years ago an old woman went into the Sudder Udalut, Bombay, at noon, when the Court was sitting; she carried a small lamp alight. When questioned as to her reason, she said she was advised that there was so much darkness in that Court, that even the small amount of light she supplied might be useful.

O British public, you are at present very much in the dark about the snakes, you may be considered as representing the worshipful Court, and here you have the old woman, and these pages are the lamp.

CHAPTER II.

According to a return published in January 1878, 22,000 lives were lost by snake-bites in India. Many to whom the subject of snakes is distasteful, and who care to know nothing of their peculiarities of structure, habits, &c., may yet be interested in knowing that efforts have been made for many years, in fact since 1855 in Sind, 1856 in the rest of the Western Presidency, to prevent the awful sacrifice of life and to reduce the mortality, not only from snake-bites, but also from wild beasts, hydrophobia, and other preventible causes. The magnitude of the first will be understood (allowing for variations in particular districts, it appears that deaths from snake-bites are more than five and a half (some returns show six) times as many as from wild beasts and hydrophobia together.

Before entering on the subject of Western India, it may be necessary to make some reference to the general return for all India—not without misgiving from want of knowledge.

It appears, however, there is the same irregularity in the geographical distribution all over India.

Why in one district, with no apparent difference in climate, or in area and population, there should be ten times as many deaths in one as compared with another, is not intelligible.

Again, there is the same apparent irregularity in action as regards efforts to reduce the mortality—most energetic in some districts, none at all in others.

It seems that the mortality is heavier in some districts than in any part of Western India.

Mortality from Snakes.

The return of—

1869 gives 14,529.
1871 „ 18,078, including wild animals.
1877 „ 19,695,* „ „

---

* 16,777 snakes; 2,918 wild animals; total, 19,695.

All India—

1875, snakes killed, 270,185.
1876, „ 212,371.
1875, total deaths by snakes and wild animals, 21,000.
1876, ditto, 15,000.

Punjaub—

1875, total deaths by snakes and wild animals, 723.
1876, ditto, 666.
1875, snakes destroyed, 144,542.
1876, „ 21,285.

The Official Report contains this explanation: "The unusually high floods of 1875 afforded greater facilities for the destruction of snakes, which were driven on to the high roads and exposed places." The reader will recognise a remarkable coincidence going back more than two thousand years.

Arrian, quoting Nearchus, stated that many snakes were destroyed by the floods of the Hydaspes, otherwise the country would have been deserted.

Punjaub (continued), 1876—

Sealkote, 17 deaths; 11,471 snakes killed.
Lahore, 72 " ; 5,054 "
Hissar, 20 " ; 1,809 "

In eighteen districts of the Punjaub, no snakes reported as killed; in the other districts the mortality varies from 50 to 639.

Lowest in Punjaub—Gurgaon, 13.
Kohat, 1.

Madras Presidency, 1876. No reward paid for the destruction of snakes.

Total killed in the whole Presidency, 532.

Deaths, highest—Tanjore, 728.
South Arcot, 80.
Salem, 86.

One very remarkable Return deserves special notice.

1875—Bangalore: 1 death; snakes killed, 1,694; rewards paid (probably by municipality), 475.

North-west Provinces and Oude:—

Rohilkund: deaths, 620; snakes killed, 482.

Benares: (highest) deaths, 871; snakes killed, none.

Fyzabad: deaths, 455; snakes killed, none.

Kumaun: (lowest) deaths, 46.

Bengal:—

Midnapore: deaths, 537; snakes killed, 6,484.

Nuddea: (highest) deaths, 700; snakes killed, 342.

Moozuferpoor: deaths, 430; snakes killed, 2,869.

Calcutta: (lowest) deaths, 16.

All India appears to have killed 270,185 in 1875, 212,371 in 1876. Rutnagherry killed 140,828 in 1876.

If there is no error in the returns, or in making this abstract, this fact is simply astounding, and certainly deserves further consideration.

Chief Secretary, Bombay, says in Report 177 of 1876, "Hitherto science has failed to discover any remedy for snake-bite," which we, with no want of respect, emphatically deny, because such an opinion, proceeding from a high official, would be productive of serious misapprehension, if allowed to pass uncontradicted.

The whole question is sufficiently involved, there are quite enough difficulties and doubts to be reconciled. The superfluous introduction of a fresh element of error is to be deplored. We must not attempt to go beyond the Snake Poison Commission and their judgment; but certain as it is that they have not up to the present time (with some hope for the future), found a remedy for cobra poison, so certain is it that there are remedies for the poison of other snakes.

Without again disturbing the repose of the Marsi or the Macedonians, more recent evidence will suffice to prove the case.

The *Echis carinata* is not known in Bengal, but is the chief agent of destruction in Western India—considered by Dr. Imlach in Scinde and others in Rutnagherry as the most destructive of the tribe of poisonous reptiles. The Chief Secretary's own records will show from Report published by the Bombay Sanitary Commission, 1864, the following recoveries from snake-bite :—

Surat	1	
Kairah	6	
Sattarah	2	
Dharwar	16	
Rutnagherry	106	
Canara	1	—132

Note particularly Appendix as regards recoveries, and also an enormous destruction of snakes, 1872.

Without further discussion on the point, perhaps this will be received as sufficient proof that there are remedies for the poison of other snakes.

The Bangalore returns for 1875 deserve very particular notice. That snakes existed in considerable numbers is proved by the fact that 1,694 snakes were killed, and there was only one death from snake-bite.

It is absolutely impossible to over-estimate the value of the service done by the Municipality or other joint authorities of Bangalore, setting a bright example which ought to be followed by every municipality in India. What has been effected at Bangalore can be done everywhere else if the same energy and good judgment are exercised. Within a certain area of every cantonment and every village, no snake should be suffered to exist. Formerly old walls, patches of milk bush, &c., were tolerated—it was, perhaps, no one's particular business to remove them,—village fences of cactus, if perfect, formed an excellent protection, not only against thieves, but also against wolves and other wild beasts; but if imperfect (broken with many paths), these hedges, useless for protection, were simply harbouring-places for snakes, and being close to and all round the villages, were a great source of danger.

But these, important as matters of detail, can only be dealt with by the local officers. *Whatever steps* were taken by the municipality of Bangalore have resulted *in a signal success of the highest importance, supplying a fulcrum* which the authorities can use all over India to meet any cavil or objection, or half-hearted pretence for doing nothing—*Bangalore has done it,* and YOU MUST.

From the Himalayas to Cape Comorin, many thousand centres or agencies exist, all of which should be employed to put down this gigantic evil—viz., Preventible Mortality from poisonous snakes.

CHAPTER III.

The following is an abbreviated copy of a letter which the Government ordered to be published (date wanting, probably 1858). The commencement of the letter regards hydrophobia, and will be found in Part II.

The deaths from snake-bites in this Presidency in the last year are given below. It appears that 575 lives have been sacrificed from snake-bites. Attention has not till recently been drawn to the loss of human life in this Presidency from this cause, though the destruction of snakes has been a recognised necessity in Scinde since 1855.

	Deaths.
Rutnagherry . .	257
Sattara . . .	69
Kaira . . .	45
Dharwar . .	40
Ahmedabad . .	27
Tannah . . .	25
Surat . . .	23
Poonah . . .	22
Khandesh . .	17
Belgaum . .	16
Broach . . .	15
Ahmednuggur .	10
Sholapoor . .	9
Total . .	575

The mortality from snake-bites, it will be seen,* is within a fraction six times greater than from hydrophobia; it is very remarkable to note that in the Zillah of Rutnagherry the mortality is half that of the whole Presidency. The Rutnagherry Zillah contains 4,500 square miles, population 665,238; the rest of the Presidency, 71,308 square miles, population 7,791,155, according to Sir G. Clerk's census.

* See Part II.

Scinde, contains 63,599 square miles, and a population of 1,071,908. The number of persons who died in Scinde in one year is estimated at 300.* On 63 inquests in a district comprising one-fifth of the whole, the mortality, therefore, is beyond measure greater in Rutnagherry than in Scinde.†

It will also appear that, whereas the people in Rutnagherry, under the pressure of the calamity, when roused to exertion by the reward, destroyed the snakes in incredible numbers; in other zillahs, where there is still a considerable loss of life, the stimulus of reward produced *no effect whatever*. For instance, Kaira, 45 deaths—reward claimed, one rupee, one anna, and six pies; Poonah, 22 deaths—reward claimed, two rupees, two annas.

In November last, it was proposed to graduate the rewards on the principle of maintaining the maximum of inducement where the people appeared unwilling to destroy snakes,

---

* This estimate is from the Scinde reports; it is evidently inaccurate, and can only be taken as an approximation.

† The mortality was probably much underrated at that time; now one subdivision (Hyderabad) enjoys a bad pre-eminence, worse than Rutnagherry at its worst with other bad districts added.

and lowering it wherever, on the contrary, a smaller reward was found to suffice.

It is to be inferred that the prejudices of the native district officers in some cases have led them, to say the least, not to afford a zealous co-operation. *There was the same scale of reward offered everywhere at the beginning.* The destruction at Rutnagherry was enormous; at Kaira, as already noticed, only seven snakes were killed.

The circular to the magistrates, of the 20th December last, noted the snakes which are decidedly poisonous. Of the greater number, the poison acts on the nervous system, and some are said to be more rapidly fatal than even the *cobra.* (More recent experiments have proved that this is an error, and that no snake exists in India with poison more rapidly fatal than the cobra.) The effect of the poison of the *foorsa* has already been described as acting on the blood. This is recognised by Dr. Morehead. The oozing of blood from the skin, &c., is also established by the late Dr. Forbes.*

---

* Some consider that the bite of no snake is necessarily fatal, if treated immediately. The poison of those which

2

Dr. Morehead notes a condition analagous to that which is present, "in advanced stages of scurvy, in which disease it is doubtless dependent on the altered constitution of the blood." As resulting from the bite of another snake, there are symptoms of altered condition in the blood in a still more aggravated form, which appears to be analagous to the conditions found in leprosy.

The Government fully recognise the necessity of guarding life in one district as in another; it is difficult, however, to imagine such a condition of things, or to picture the general consternation in England, or here in Bombay,* if among 665,000 souls, 257 deaths occurred from snake-bites in one year.

Considering its area, Kaira, with 45 deaths, presents a worse condition than Sattara, with 69 deaths. We may expect to find many snakes in a jungle district, but it is remarkable to note

---

act less rapidly on the system produce the most horrible effects.

* In Bombay, with a population of 500,000, 14 deaths have occurred in five years, very important as proving the possibility of extermination.

the great number in the most highly cultivated district in Western India, and that the rewards offered have produced no result.

There stands the terrible record for the whole Presidency :—

575 deaths from snake-bites.
105 deaths from hydrophobia.

Total 680 lives lost from preventible causes in one year.

Something has been done to diminish the mortality from both these causes. To believe it cannot be diminished would be equivalent to believing that wolves have not been exterminated in England, or that snakes still swarm in Bombay as at Rutnagherry.

In conformity with the orders of Government, circulars have been sent to the magistrates lowering the rewards. If it is found expedient to offer higher rewards in Guzerat, and if the injunctions of the magistrates to the district officers fail to produce effect, a separate report will be submitted to Government.

Snakes killed in the Rutnagherry district alone:—

December	.	142,830
January .	.	31,066
February	.	2,119

This ends the abbreviated Report, and conveys a correct idea of what the question was in 1858.

CHAPTER IV.

We proceed to give some particulars regarding Western India as it is now, though the task is anything but easy. There is much difficult to explain, and some palpable error to contend with.

But it is in no spirit of fault-finding these observations are made, except as regards those who without knowledge or experience have propounded or countenanced wild theories or opinions which, left without emphatic contradiction, would paralyse every effort at reform.

Our experience, at any rate, goes back to a very remote date: whether that experience carries with it any corresponding amount of knowledge, the reader will judge for himself. We profess to supply *facts* backed by authority, and give prominence to certain points referred to in the text, viz.:

1st. The general disbelief in the amount of mortality shown in the returns.

2nd. The opinion that a great proportion of the mortality is to be attributed to secret poisoning, falsely assigned to snakes.

3rd. The grave error that there is no remedy for snake-poison.

We deny each, and trust to prove these are mischievous delusions.

The snake best known in name and appearance is the *Cobra capella*, but in Western India another snake takes precedence as a destructive agent, the *Echis carinata* (known as Kupper in Sind, Foorsa in Concan, Malabar, and Ceylon, Afaie at Delhi, Horatta Pam in Telingana, Viryen Pam in the Tamul country). This snake is not known in Bengal, in fact it disappears at some point near Vizagapatam; from thence till the neighbourhood of Delhi it does not exist. On the other hand, from Delhi to the south-west, through the Punjaub, Sind, the Concan, and Malabar coast to Ceylon, the *Echis carinata* is found, and everywhere holds the same bad pre-eminence as a destroyer of life.

When a snake is not killed, or at any rate seen distinctly, there is always a doubt as to identity, except by the peculiar symptoms—the poison of certain snakes, notably the cobra, produces coma and speedy death, whereas the poison of others, Russell's viper for example, produces excessive pain, convulsions, vomiting, &c.

Old writers as well as modern authorities agree (with wide discrepancies on other points) as regards some of these symptoms as following the bite of snakes, but speedy death is not the attribute of the cobra alone, nor is Russell's viper the only reptile whose poison produces great suffering. This is alluded to as serving to illustrate the main point under consideration, which is *that the poison of the Echis carinata produces effects which cannot be mistaken.* Ancient writers called this snake *Hæmorrois,* and fully recognised its deadly character.

Drs. Morchead, Leith, Forbes, all identify the foorsa of the Concan with *Echis carinata.* Dr. Imlach, who was in Sind, pronounced this snake, there called "kupper," as the most deadly snake in Sind; presumably that being most numerous, it killed even more than the fatal cobra.

Official returns of several hundred deaths in 1857–1858 show that some occurred in one hour, few survived twelve hours, but the *Echis carinata* poison, though, without speedy and judicious treatment, almost certain death, allowed the patient to linger as long as eight or nine days, or an average of four or five days, and *presented also the very remarkable symptom of blood oozing in small spots through the skin.*

Thus it will be seen that the slow action of the poison, and the oozing of blood through the pores, do mark and sufficiently *distinguish the poison of the Echis carinata from that of any other snake.*

It is referred to in Arian in one of the fragments of Nearchus. "On the banks of the Hydaspes Nearchus is surprised at the multitude and the noxious nature of the tribe of reptiles. They retreat from the plains at the period of inundations (precisely as they do now in the Concan at the commencement of the rainy season), and enter the houses. The minuteness of some is a cause of danger, because it is difficult to guard against their attacks."

Aristobulus wrote that "None of these, however, are so noxious as the slender small serpents (a span long) which are found concealed in tents, in vessels, and in hedges. Persons wounded by them *bleed from every pore*, suffering great pain, and die unless they have immediate assistance; but this is easily obtained by means of the virtues of Indian roots and drugs."

It is evident the Macedonians considered the native doctors, or "sophisti," as they termed them, had efficient remedies, which now are not known or not recognised; with a reservation.*

Diodorus Siculus and Lucan repeat the same opinion as already given, and Cuvier assigned its proper character to *Echis carinata*, and most clearly distinguished this reptile from *Vipera communis*, alias *Pelias berus*, which is the English viper, and does not exist in India.

Recent inquiry has been made to clear up a doubt as to an alleged dangerous viper in Norway,† but this proves to be the same (*Vipera communis*) as the viper of the New

* The persons bitten died without treatment. The Macedonians found people who understood treatment. The doctors at Rutnagherry do the same.

† Vide Appendix.

Forest, &c., the poison producing much pain and other disagreeable effects, but *not* death.

Prince Max von Weid found in Brazil about the same proportion of poisonous to harmless snakes as Dr. Russell on the Coromandel coast—about seven as compared to forty harmless.

There is an important point which may now be considered. Many persons hold that the returns of deaths by snake-bites are inaccurate, and that under the veil of snake-bite other deaths are to be looked for—domestic tragedies, deaths of wives by husbands, or husbands by wives, from jealousy. That such things may have occurred is possible, but it must be reduced to its lowest term.

The wilder tribes—Bheels, Kolies, &c.—are, as a rule, exemplary in their domestic relations, as in courage, truthfulness, and fidelity; all qualities in which some other classes are so lamentably wanting. If a Kolie thought his wife unfaithful, he would most probably kill her, and tell everyone he had done it, but it would never occur to him to say she had died of snake-bite.

Again, among the Mahomedans jealousy in a harem is a very old story, and poison is often spoken of, with what foundation or to what extent is beyond the present question, only that it helps us so far, if we consider for a moment how very difficult it would be to *pretend a case of snake-poison**—in some the lethargy and speedy death, in others prolonged torture and extreme suffering.

It was not the opinion of Dr. Imlach, who was in Sind, and to whom the credit is due as the first to warn the Government through the Commissioner, Mr. Frere.

It was not the opinion of the police; the magistrates considered that all cases were not reported. But as the returns were prepared by their own subordinates, the native district officers, it is to be presumed, as much care was taken as with any other sort of reports, sharp reprimand followed any carelessness. *Finally, deaths from pretended snake-bites would occur at all times of the year.* People of India are not yet acquainted with the statistics of snake-poison. A learned Calcutta baboo may understand the characteristics of *serpa visha*, but among the masses, not one in many thou-

* It must be remembered that it is the sufferer who has to feign these symptoms.

sand knows auything more than that eobra-poison is eertain death (with the exeeption of the python, the roek-snake, and one or two others). He firmly believes all snakes are poisonous, whereas the faet is that in Western India only the following seven are eertainly poisonous, and were identified by Dr. Leith, differently named in Guzerat, the Deeean, and Canarese distriets: *Naya tripudians, Echis carinata, Bothrops viridis, Daboia elegans, Dipsas trigonata, Bungarus cœruleus, Pelamis bicolor,* and other varieties of sea-snake.

These six are eertainly harmless:—*Oodria* or *Tropidonatus piscator, Tropidonatus stolatus, Lycodon lebe, Lycodon nympha, Lycodon aulicum, Coriphodon Biumenbachii.* There are some doubtful snakes.

Deaths *from pretended snake-bites would occur at all times of the year,* but it is a matter of absolute eertainty that *more deaths occur in the three hottest months than in all the rest of the year.* If a man, therefore, were jealous of his wife he would hardly wait from November till May; if he wanted to kill her, he would find vegetable poisons within a short distanee of his door. Why, then, sham a snake-bite? People have died, and there may have been suspicious circumstances, and the allegation of snake-bite may not have been fully credited; but these cases must be so rare that, multiplied many times over, they would not affect the returns. Moreover, if such cases were frequent, they would appear in the records of the police and the criminal courts, but, as mentioned elsewhere, two magistrates* of long experience concur in stating not only that no such case ever came before them, but they never heard of one in any other district. How or from whom the notion has emanated is not clear, but it is a mischievous delusion.

If, when the returns were first called for in 1856, there was room for doubt as to accuracy, the fact remains that the Government of India (and it is to be presumed that the Government of India consider, with the reservation of incompleteness, their returns to be correct) announce a mortality of 22,000 in 1876, twenty years after. This, of course, for the whole continent; but in the district of Rutnagherry or South Concan—area 5,808, population 665,238—there were 250 deaths in the year 1856.

---

* Since this was written, another magistrate states he has heard of such a case, but none ever came before him.

If a tithe of such mortality occurred in England from snake-bites, or hydrophobia, or other preventible cause, very speedy and effectual measures would be adopted.

It has recently been stated that the mortality in Rutnagherry has been reduced to thirty. If this be correct it is a fact of the utmost importance, as proving that it is possible to exterminate snakes if only an efficient agency be employed. The failure in Guzerat proves nothing beyond the fact that a system unsuited to the province (under a strong but covert opposition) necessarily failed.

CHAPTER V.

SOMEONE remarked, in connection with the New Zealander sitting on the broken arch of London Bridge—of whom everyone is so tired and wishes most sincerely that for the future he should be relegated to Gloucester Bridge to join his fellow idiot, who, according to Sidney Smith, used to employ his time like Molière's French Viscount—"*qui s'occupe en crachant dans l'eau pour faire des rondes.*"

This New Zealander, according to some *mauvais plaisant*, is supposed to have gone to India after the extinction of our rule, and found nothing to mark the fact that the English had ever been in India but "empty bottles." It is to be hoped our readers are not of that persuasion.

They may be reminded that at different periods famines have desolated great tracts of country, and that no Hindoo Rajah or Emperor of Delhi —not even the very highest impersonation of royalty, the great Padshah Akbar—ever attempted to fight against famine.

The Pindarees have been put down, and the Thugs and the Bengal Dacoits; the Marquis of Hastings and a costly war destroyed the power of the Pindarees; Colonel Sleeman annihilated the Thugs, and Elphinstone Jackson the Dacoits; but 22,000 lives are still lost by snakes annually, and usurers eat the hearts of the cultivators. Something, therefore, still remains to be done.

In the Bombay Presidency the deaths from snake-bites were—1856, 575; 1857, 446 1858, 368. Difference between the first and third year 207, proving that a reduction is practicable with continued effort.

Referring to what is noted elsewhere about the mortality in the hot months,* it appears

---

* Some have compared the four hottest with the eight other months, which is an improvement, and would show a still stronger contrast in Guzerat and Sind, where the hot weather lasts longer than at Rutnagherry.

from a return of 1857 that there were 316 deaths between June and November; between December and May, 111; in the two hottest months, June and July, 136; in December and January, 30.

Something might here be added about treatment. There have been snake-charmers or snake-doctors in every age of the world from ancient Egypt to the back-woods of North America. Their existence shows they secured some measure of belief in their power to effect cures; but the action of the poison of some snakes, notably the cobra, is so rapid that if there is the slightest delay in applying the remedies the sufferer is past hope. There is the widest divergence of opinion on this point. Some hold that a ligature applied and the holes of the bite laid open with a knife or lancet, followed by strong doses of ammonia, will savc life, but wc must be prepared for objections such as whether thc full amount of poison was interceptcd by the clothes or otherwise, or whether by chance the snake had previously bitten some other object. Two instances may be quoted which are prccisely oppositc. A Malee (native gardcner) at Poonah, was bitten by a cobra, and had the presence of mind himself to chop off the wounded finger. It would have been very satisfactory to record that his courage was rewarded and that his life was saved, but he died. Captain L——, of the Second Queen's, was bitten in the thumb by a cobra. He applied a ligature and cut open the wounds, drank a large dose of raw brandy, which (being a very temperate man) produced its full beneficial effect; he walked instead of rode into camp. He met the doctor (who had been sent for from camp to meet him), and told him that the whole College of Physicians could not have done more for him than he had done for himself; he lived many years after.

Perhaps if the Malee had had the brandy and had walked some miles at a rapid pace in a state of profuse perspiration, he might have lived.

It appears, in a common-sense view of the matter, that to put on a ligature and to puncture the wound is to be commended, and that if done at once some of the poison must be arrested.

Some of the poison must be intercepted, and something less than the quantity needed to destroy life may be absorbed.* It is supposed that the bite of a mad dog through cloth may in some cases prove harmless, the passage of the teeth through a tolerably thick material serving to arrest and retain the virus.

But in cases of snake-bite, where swelling is a marked symptom, to retain the ligature is found to aggravate the pain to an unbearable degree, and in *Echis carinata* bite the puncture accelerates the hæmorrhage.

Dr. Morehead mentions three cases of phoorsa bite at Mahabaleshwar. He found it impracticable to retain the ligature, and the hæmorrhage from the puncture was excessively difficult to arrest. In one case, that of a Parsee woman, there was recovery, though ammonia was the only remedy.

B—— mentions a case in Java in which, consequent on the pain from swelling, the ligature was removed, the man died immediately; this was a cobra.

Ancients and moderns used the ligature, and in cases like the cobra, where the action of the poison is exceedingly rapid, it may be found to

---

* Report of Snake Poison Commission shows that a very small quantity of cobra poison will destroy life; but this does not necessarily apply to the poison of other snakes.

be indispensable; but in other cases, where it produces great swelling, it produces great suffering.

There are some interesting particulars, perfectly intelligible to non-professionals, regarding the phoorsa and its poison in Dr. Morehead's second volume, page 702, chap. 22, of which two extracts:—"The effect of the phoorsa poison is clearly on the blood, nor is it very speedily induced." "The hæmorrhagic tendency is due to the altered state of the blood; the facts now recorded differ from the description of snake-bites in general."

Dr. Forbes, adverting to the worst forms of fever, in which a malignant and hæmorrhagic character were well marked, was reminded of the effects in two cases of snake-bite which he had witnessed.

Dr. M——, a celebrated geologist and naturalist, travelled from Surat to Kandish, through the Dang, in the month of January, at which time the forest is not safe. He caught the jungle fever and died at Palusanair. He had the symptom, oozing of blood through the pores of the skin, to a marked degree. It ap-appears to be the opinion of medical authorities that this symptom is not common, but it has been noticed by Drs. Morehead, Forbes, and others, and is *not* petechiæ.

This snake—phoorsa or *Echis carinata*—has very peculiar characteristics. One is, it appears to have no fear of the approach of man, will not avoid the path, and there is always great risk of treading on this reptile unawares, when it instantly attacks.

It has also been remarked by Dr. Imlach and others that this snake has a very peculiar and malignant expression. Old writers have noticed the same. The physician Jonstonus, in his description of this snake as the hemorrhois, writes:—"*Oculis igneo quodam fulgore ardentibus*"—for identity—"*Is enim in eo tractu quo Alexander Porum persequebatur inventos fuisse serpentes parvos quidem—ad eorumque morsum toto corpore sanguineum sudorem dimanasse.*"

Cuvier, referring to the rattle-snake, observes that these snakes are most dangerous where the country and the season are hottest, but that the nature of that snake is not aggressive, though the poison is so deadly (*l'atrocité de son venin*) as to occasion death in a few minutes. This applies to the Indian season as already noted, and also to the character of the cobra, which merits equally to be qualifed as "*tranquille et Engourdi.*"

The *Trigonocephalus* is just the opposite; attacks without provocation. *Bothrops viridis*, or *Trimersure*, belongs to this class, and the *Tic polonga** has long been considered very aggressive, and attacks the cobra. Wood, quoting Sir Emerson Tennant, mentions that the judge of Trincomalee was compelled in 1858 to leave his house by *Tic polongas.*

C. Owen, D.D., 1742, wrote, "When the noya (cobra) and polonga meet, they fight till one be killed. The conqueror eats up the slain."

These may be taken to represent two kinds of reptiles—the first, though possessing deadly power in the highest degree, not disposed to use it except under great provocation; the other always ready to attack.

Craspedocephalus is fortunately not found in India, but Cuvier states "Ici vient le Trimer sure vert de Lacepede ou Boodroo pam Russell." Dr. R., however, states "the poison of the Boodroo pam appears to be less deleterious and slower than those of the cobra or the *Tic polonga*, and in some respects different."

---

* Daboia, or Russell's viper.

Subsequent experiments have probably modified that judgment to bring the reptile up to the standard assigned to it by Lacep, Fitzing, or P. Max v. Wied. The opinion of Van der Hoven on this matter was, "*The bite of all venomous snakes is not equally dangerous to man. In some cases the poison shows itself at a very short interval;* death occurs after violent spasms and other nervous symptoms, and decomposition follows death with extraordinary rapidity."

Cuvier writes in substance as follows:—"In addition to these two tribes of serpents, properly so called, a third has lately been recognised, in which the organisation and armature of the jaws are nearly the same as in non-venomous serpents, but where the first maxillary tooth, larger than the others, is perforated for the transmission of poison, as in venomous serpents with isolated fangs. These serpents form two genera—*Bungarus* and *Hydrus*."

The fact is curious. Snakes, drawn and characterised with great accuracy by Russell in 1796, were described by Cuvier as novelties in 1816.

This explanation is necessary to show, in the first place, that the four snakes, *Echis carinata*, cobra, *Tic polonga*, and the green viper or *Boodroo pam*—the snakes to which are rightly ascribed the chief mortality—are easily recognised by anyone with the least experience.

But the fifth, of which, in consideration of its importance, Cuvier's description is given. This snake, unfortunately, resembles the harmless lycodon.

Some snakes which are found in Bengal do not exist in Western India: *Bungarus fascialus*, &c. Dr. Leith does not appear to have found *Elaps ophiophagus* among those submitted for his inspection. If it exists it is fortunately not common, being a most formidable reptile of great size—deadly as the cobra, with the aggressive character of *Craspedocephalus*.

CHAPTER VI.

MEN of high authority consider that much money has been thrown away in giving rewards tor the destruction of harmless snakes. This grievous error arose from ignorance or carelessness, but, in this particular instance, not without excuse, on account of the real difficulty of discriminating between *Bungarus cæruleus*, a deadly snake, and *Lycodon aulicus*, which is perfectly harmless.

The estimate of mortality from *Bungarus cæruleus* is subject to correction. Both this and the *hydrus*, or *Pelamis bicolor*, are very deadly snakcs, but, judging from thc Returns, the percentage of deaths assigned to thcm appears to be small. The venom, indeed, if not so rapid, appears, without treatment, to be nearly as deadly as that of the cobra.

It is safe to conclude that all snakes found in salt water in India are poisonous. A notable instance of mistake as to the character of a snake occurred many years ago on board a ship in Madras Roads.* One was taken up in a bucket, and under the impression (general at that time) that water-snakes were harmless, this reptile was handled by one of the crew, who was bitten and died.

Though a cure for the poison of the cobra, owing to the extreme rapidity of the action of the poison, may often be despaired of, yet to believe there is no remedy for the bite of other snakes cannot be justified; it is opposed to a great mass of evidence, ancient and modern. The point is so important as to justify some detail.

Bell, Wood, Bruce, and other recent writers, Max von Wied, Van der Hoeven, Russell, 1798; Owen, 1742; Jonstonus, a Dutch physician, who wrote in 1657.

* Great numbers of snakes may be seen in the Straits of Malacca, some swimming half erect like cobras, others flat on the water.

Psylli and Marsi, professional snake-doctors, accompanied the Roman army in Lybia; Crates, of Pergamos; Varro, Agathereides, Lucan, are quoted as authorities about the *Psylli* at Syrenaica, and Marmorica, in Africa, and also at Parcum, in the Hellespont. Note again the Macedonians on the banks of the Hydaspes.

Is it reasonable to suppose that all were imposed upon by false pretenders to a knowledge of cures which had no existence? Their admission of their own ignorance, and preference of the natives of the country (as on the Hydaspes), may be taken as strong proofs of good faith, and their admissions of frequent failure make statements of success more credible.

When cholera occurs with almost immediate collapse, such a case is beyond treatment. In like manner the bite of a cobra in the hot season, in or near a vein, is probably as certain death as cholera with collapse.

But as with spasmodic cholera so with snake-bites: under more favourable conditions a fair proportion of recoveries may be expected from judicious treatment. In some cases of snake-bite and cholera there is no hope, but in other cases, under more favourable circumstances, lives *may be saved under treatment which would be lost without treatment.*

Unless history ancient and modern is to be regarded as worthless, lives have been saved by remedies of some sort. Modern science and medical knowledge may be expected to discover more potent and suitable remedies.

It is idle to say we have heard this before. If the facts are not understood or not appreciated, if they are disputed, or if no sufficient action has been taken, repetition is necessary. *Nunquam nimis dicitur quod nunquam satis dicitur.*

More difficult works have been accomplished in India at which men through all time will look back with astonishment. Forts deemed impregnable taken; great battles fought against incredible odds, with arms which would now be regarded as worse than bows and arrows (a matchlock was more accurate than an old flint-musket, and had a longer range).

Since Plassey, one long chapter of impossibilities made possible (as before stated, Pindarees, Thugs, Bengal Dacoits), the people of the time were told to hold back and not meddle with suttee or infanticide—not to offend the prejudices of the natives; for the same reason at one time it was difficult and dangerous to kill snakes and mad dogs. Now we are considered quixotic and absurd to expect success in exterminating snakes.* (*We* means Indians, from the Viceroy to the Boots at the Swan, late full private in —— Regiment. Boots, with much abuse, still feels interested in India.) People must not forget *we* have just come out damaged, but victorious, in a struggle with famine — an infinitely more difficult matter than this snake question.

As to extermination (without going back to wolves in England, but keeping to snakes in India), there were as many snakes in Bombay as elsewhere in the Concan in the last century. The surgeon of Admiral Watson's flag-ship, Mr. Ives, is an authority. He mentions six different sorts of deadly snakes found at Bombay at that time, 1773.

A marked diminution was obtained in the

---

* Vice Roy and Boots at the Swan, Zenith and Nadir—
"To win but thy smile were I Sardanapalus,
I'd descend from my throne and be Boots at an ale 'us."
Ingoldsby Leg.

years 1857, 1858, and 1859, under Lord Elphinstone's government, as before stated. But Rutnagherry supplies the most important and absolutely conclusive proof of all, seeing that *a mortality of* 250 *has been reduced to thirty in twenty years.* The possibility of exterminating snakes may with this evidence be considered established. What has been done in the Rutnagerry district may be done elsewhere with an efficient agency.

When Captain Outram (afterwards General Sir James) commanded the Bheel Corps, in Khandish, tigers swarmed. Any one who had then predicted that the tigers would ever be exterminated, or even become scarce, would have been considered a lunatic, but Khandish men now go for tigers to Central India.

The present object is to popularise the subject, to draw attention to its importance, with the view of obtaining a practical result, viz., a decrease in the present enormous amount of preventible mortality in India. References to existing authorities are avoided as much as possible, more particularly as their opinions are in antagonism.

However herpetologists may differ on other points, they will agree with the unlearned on the main point, that 22,000 persons ought not to die every year from snake-bite if it can in any way be shown that there are means of any sort, not involving an unreasonable and impossible expenditure, by which the mortality may be materially reduced.

Many facts and inferences here set forth might be disputed or rejected on the ground of improbability if not supported by official record, or in other cases by recognised high authority. As long as one can quote Cuvier or Dr. Morehead and others already named, one need fear no adverse criticism, except on the ground of injudicious inferences.

The reader, however, will be good enough to remember that this paper does not pretend to anything more than to supply some information in the form of notes roughly tacked together. An exhaustive treatment of so great a question—not snakes for the herpetologist, but for the police, snakes as representing assassins or Thugs, or other professional murderers—cannot be attempted in these limits; but the purpose is answered if attention is more specially drawn to facts not generally known, connected with this great and constant source of danger to life to which the people of India (after all that has been done in other ways for their welfare and safety) are still subject.

As to the "official record," in addition to what has been already stated, it is worthy of notice that when adverse critics dispute the return of mortality set down as 22,000, and reject it as an exaggeration, would they be satisfied if, for the sake of argument, it were conceded (though in the opposite sense) that the return may be taken as an approximation?

It is also to be remembered that to affect the numbers to any appreciable extent (to make a false return) many district officers between Delhi and Cape Comorin must combine, and continue to combine, and their successors also, through a series of years. Anyone with any knowledge of India will see at once that this is an absurd conclusion. Many (of course, *not* district officers) have combined, in many forms, to cheat the Government, but there has always been some prospect of advantage or profit.

But to *exaggerate the Returns of Mortality would be entirely without profit*. On the contrary the higher the mortality in any particular district the greater the certainty of unfavourable comment and censure from superior officers on the just ground of want of zeal on the part of local authority in failing to abate the evil. Dealing now with probabilities, the result is just the other way. If deaths (as has been alleged on good authority) from one cause or other are not registered, the obvious result is that the real mortality is greater than reported.

The improbabilities are not limited to this much disputed Return. What more improbable than that in two conterminous districts in Gujerat—Ahmedabad, area 4,399, Kaira, 1,274—the mortality in the lesser, Kaira, 60, should be nearly twice that of the greater, 36; or that in the same Kaira (the smallest district in the presidency) there should be a greater mortality, 60 (return of 1857), than in the whole of the Deccan (56 deaths); or that in the country south of the Krishna, in one district—Dharwar, 33, or more than Khandish, Poonah, and Sholapore put together; or again, that the mortality in Rutnagerry should be more than half the whole of the presidency; or most astonishing of all, that this mortality should be reduced in 1864 to 94, and in 1877 to 30? Moreover, there were 106 recoveries in 1864, In 1857 a recovery was so rare as to be scarce hoped for—in fact, the records of that period showed none.

CHAPTER VII.

At the risk of being considered tedious ("as tedious as a king," according to Dogberry) it is necessary to quote from and compare some other returns to prove very important facts. While great energy, as shown in a particular district, has produced magnificent results, on the other hand the mortality has increased in other parts of the presidency.

Taking Kaira again, the mortality in 1857 was 60; in 1869, 85; in 1870, 100. In Rutnagherry the mortality, which had been 250 in 1856, was reduced to 53 in 1869; rose again to 86 in 1870; and in 1875 to 144; again reduced to 30 in 1877.

If time and space admitted, if many more

records were examined and compared, the whole question could be presented in a more complete form, but it does not appear that the general result would be affected by such labour, involving also long delay, or further by adding a comparison of mortality to population, instead of area, or of adding more figures of any kind. For it suffices to prove there is a great mortality from snakes, which is susceptible of reduction everywhere, and which has been in certain districts reduced in a very remarkable manner. Some think (perhaps with reason) the whole question hinges on the point whether it is or is not possible in any way, by any sort of measure, to reduce the mortality. The operations at Rutnagherry *prove the affirmative, and the intermitting periods of disaster prove an abatement of energetic action only.*

The aggregate mortality in the Guzerat and coast districts is enormously in excess of the whole of the rest of the presidency, and the mortality in the districts south of the Bheema is much in excess of the whole of the Deccan.

So far from presuming directly or indirectly to impute blame, it may be broadly stated that the Government in this matter have had to contend with many great difficulties, of which not the least are financial, but there has been opposition, not the less effective for being covert, and it should be distinctly understood that when the attention of Government was first drawn to the subject there was most generous and hearty support in initiating the measure, and without that support it must have collapsed.

Since then there have apparently been doubt and discouragement from unsatisfactory results; these again arising from many causes, adverse and hostile opinions, insufficient and unsuitable agency, feeble, half-hearted, and incompetent agents, and, again and again to be repeated, *strong, though covert, ooposition.* Many efforts have been made, not always wise or well directed; much money has been spent, sometimes well spent and with appreciable results, at other times wasted in killing harmless snakes.

But the only true test which can or ought to bc accepted is still wanting. Till there is a large diminution in the rate of mortality all that has yet been done can only be taken as an instalment.

There is no present prospect of being able to "rest and be thankful"; the work must be vigorous and persistent—such work as has been done at Rutnagerry *without the intermissions and disastrous results of increased mortality* before noticed. The returns plainly show when there has been any abatement of vigorous action there has followed an increase of mortality.

Any suggestion is submitted with reservations, fully recognising that nothing can supply the want of local knowledge and experience; even these lose their value in the course of time, when the condition of things is altered. But some things do not alter.*

The position now is hopeful beyond anything that could have been expected twenty years ago.

Two great problems are solved. 1st. It is proved beyond a doubt that a remedy has been found for a poison† which is deadly and mortal without treatment, but which is now found to be susceptible of cure, a possibility generally disbelieved at the period referred to.

2nd. With the proof already detailed no man need hesitate to believe that to exterminate snakes is feasible, and that the still existing mor-

---

* For example:—Any remission of action formerly, as in later days, was followed by an increase of mortality.

† The poison of the *Echis carinata*.

tality is susceptible of sure decrease under an agency of some sort suited to the particular district. With resolute and persistent continued effort, and not otherwise, and no mercy on any who directly or indirectly offer opposition, covert or open—in a word, to endeavour to follow (if only like *parvus Iulus haud passibusæquis*) Colonel Sleeman's steps.

The subject is a very large one, and well deserves to be more fully reported on by some officer with more recent knowledge, who has made it a subject of serious consideration, and who can supply what is wanting in this superficial treatment, which in some sort may be considered as resembling Indian ploughing in light soil—a mere scratching of the surface. It bears, or will bear, a crop all the same.

If it were not a serious subject, involving most important considerations, the extent of incredulity would be ludicrous. It seems in so grave a matter trivial to record what men say. They utterly disbelieve the returns. It is not of the slightest use to tell them how they are prepared and revised by distinguished officials of great experience.

They say, "It is Bill's or Joe's pet crochet. Queer old bird, with his 22,000—how can he expect us to believe that? And as to old B——, he was always as mad as a hatter, and now he has got snakes on the brain."

They thrust their disbelief *en bloc,*

> Like feather-bed 'twixt castle wall,
> And heavy brunt of cannon-ball,

and argument or explanation are useless. Another remark is this: "Don't you think you should get better information, and revise the list?" If you answer, "We have already the best information, and the lists have been revised," they go into the deaf-adder line of business, and do it very well.

That snake-poison differs in virulence and character has long been a recognised fact. The table in the next page will show how great is the diversity in the symptoms produced by the poison of various kinds of snakes.

Cuvier considered the Haje, or African cobra, to be Cleopatra's snake, because it produces painless death, but it does not appear that his judgment on this point has been fully accepted.

---

* The matter is further complicated by the fact that the bite of a very small cobra or Daboia a few days old is deadly. *Judice* Sir W. E., a small deadly is not necessarily an old or full-grown small snake.

The popular notion is that Cleopatra's asp was a small snake.

The Portuguese have left a tradition at Bombay about a small snake called Cobra de Morte, which produced instant death. Russell mentions the sudden death of Governor Bourchiers Porter from the bite of a snake. It appears that the existence of Cobra de Morte requires further evidence.

The returns of 1857 and 1858 show some instances of sudden death from the bite of snakes. In 1857 three are entered as instantaneous, twelve within half an hour, forty-four within an hour; in 1858, eight instantaneous, twelve within half an hour, thirty within an hour. Some are ascribed to cobra, none to any small snake.*

Coma.—It is recognised as the peculiar characteristic of cobra-poison, Cuvier, &c. Swelling.—C. Owen, Dr. Russell, Van der Hoeven, &c. Convulsions.—Van der Hoeven, Owen, Russell, Bell, &c. Discoloration.—C. Owen and others. In the returns of 1857 there were entered these cases of discoloration :—1, Body

* *Vipera brachyura* and a minute Cuvier does not appear to have been identified in India; but the belief in the existence of a very small deadly snake is very general among the natives.

turned yellow, nails black; 2, body discoloured; 3, body discoloured; 4, body turned green and swelled; 5, body turned black, blue, and green; 6, body turned black. Hæmorrhage. —C. Owen, Russell, Vander Hoeven, and others. Leprosy.—Russell, Morehead, and others; some native writers also. Vomiting.—Bell, Russell, Owen, &c. Pains.—Burning and excessive thirst ascribed to Dipsas and other snakes. Putridity. —C. Owen, Russcll, Van der Hoeven, &c. It is evident there is not only a difference in the virulence (*l'atrocité*) of the poison, but there must be an essential difference in the quality or character to produce effects so widely differing from suddcn death in a few minutes to a prolonged illness of many days, with all the remarkablc varicty of symptoms above specified.

On further consideration, and viewing its very great importance, it is expedient to show the mortality of the four districts, Khandesh, Kaira, Sholapoor, and Rutnagherry in a more intelligible form.

According to a census taken when Sir George Clcrk was Governor, the area of the presidency (not including Sind and Canara) was—

Square miles .	80,044
Population .	8,456,393

Khandesh is the largest province.

Area (square miles)	16,597
Population .	785,091

Mortality—

1857 . . .	11
1864 . . .	17
1869 . . .	15
1870 . . .	5
1875 . . .	35

Kaira.—This is the smallest province, with the highest mortality, considering area and population:—

Area (square miles)	1,274
Population .	580,631

Mortality—

1857 . . .	60
1864 . . .	31
1869 . . .	85
1870 . . .	100
1875 . .	Return wanting.

The area of Kaira is within a fraction the same as Gloucestershire.

Sholapoor, with the lowest mortality—

Area (square miles)	10,277
Population	675,115

Mortality—

1857	9
1864	15
1869	5
1870	9
1875	7

Rutnagherry—

Area (square miles)	5,808
Population	665,238

Mortality—

1856	257
1857	65
1864	94
1869	53
1875	144
1877	30

It will be observed there is more information respecting this district. It has been the chief field of operations. The ebb and flow in the tide of mortality are worthy of observation.

This table also shows the extraordinary irregularity in the distribution of snakes, and the mortality; for example, in its worst years, the mortality of Rutnagherry is higher than Kaira; but in other years Kaira is higher, though the area of Kaira is only one-fifth of Rutnagherry, and population as 580,631 to 665,238.

CHAPTER VIII.

THERE are members of certain castes who hold very rigid and inconvenient notions on the subject of taking animal life of any sort, under any circumstances. To put such persons into positions in which they must either sacrifice their religious scruples, or else act in opposition to their duty to the Government, is very bad policy.

But the Government choice is not limited in the selection of agents; there are others, thoroughly efficient for the duties of district officers, who have no sort of prejudice of this kind, who would with equal indifference kill a cobra or any other snake. Moreover, in a lower grade there are plenty of Bheels, Bendurs, who have no scruples; and others, as the

Wudders (itinerant stone-cutters), who, if not grossly maligned, not only kill snakes, but eat them.

If rent-free lands were granted in tracts, now waste, &c., there would be in a brief time colonies of snake-destroyers in every sub-division of districts. The condition of service, that half the number should do service where required for three months only—the months of November, December, and January, or December, January, and February, according to the time in which snakes congregate in particular districts, and can therefore be killed in the grcatest numbers and with the least risk to the killer.

That snakes do migrate and congregate is a very important fact (may be taken as proved), and must materially assist those who are charged with the work of extermination. Snakes were brought in to the head-quarters at Rutnagerry—

December 1857 .	142,830
January 1858 .	31,066
February 1858 .	2,119

Rutnagerry includes Malwar and all the other stations of the Collectorate.

It is true the reward was lowered (probably in the end of December), and that, no doubt, had some effect, but it does not cover the whole question, as it will be noted 31,066 snakes were killed in January—less than a quarter of the previous month; but still a very large number, and double all the other districts for the whole year—for the whole presidency, 47,142; Rutnagerry, 31,659; balance total of all the rest, 15,483—February--2,119.

It does not appear that any were killed in March, a bot month in the Southern Concan; it is more dangerous to kill snakes than in the cold weather.

It should be particularly noticed that at the period referred to only three or four snakes were killed in the whole year, either at Kaira or Poonah, though the same rewards were offered as at Rutnagherry in the commencement.

Fortunately the officer who was then in charge of the Rutnagherry district is able to supply proof as to the incredible number of snakes killed. An abbreviation of a letter of the 14th August 1879 states:—

"I was officiating collector and magistrate of Rutnagherry in the end of 1857. At that time the orders for the destruction of snakes were in full force. The natives used to bring in the snakes to head-quarters every evening, and they were counted and chopped up to prevent the reward being claimed a second time for the same snake. I am unable, after so many years, to speak with certainty as to the number destroyed daily, but to the best of my recollection there used to be from twenty to thirty baskets, containing altogether several hundred snakes of various species, including the foorsa and the cobra. When the amount of reward was reduced, the natives refused to destroy the snakes, alleging that the remuneration was not sufficient for the risk. Snakes abounded throughout the whole of the Rutnagerry Collectorate.

"Yours,

"D. L."

This is very important as supplying evidence of a very remarkable fact, but also proving that the whole question, at all events in this instance, *was regulated—not by any religious principle, but by a certain standard of reward or tariff*, which, at one point, in the judgment of the officer administering the district, *did, and at a lower did not, command the required service.*

More than twenty years ago, when the subject was under consideration, a letter was written, to which the answer is given below, by an officer who is still on the medical staff in India.

Extract of letter from Dr. B——, written in 1858:—

"The remedy I particularly alluded to, for foorsa bite, was tannic acid. For some now unknown cause, the poison of this snake has the power of destroying the gelatinous and fibrinous particles of the blood, rendering it so watery or liquid that it readily exudes through the veins. Tannic acid possesses no specific action on the actual poison itself, but it has the power of rendering the blood less liquid by combining with the gelatinous and fibrinous portions. It is on account of its action on the blood that tannic acid is of so much use in the treatment of foorsa bites. It restores the blood in a measure to its natural condition, and there is time then to administer other remedies before death ensues. The poison of the foorsa is of so specific a nature that an analysis of it would, I am certain, be attended with good results."

It is a point of great interest to be ascertained whether the recoveries recorded as having occurred at Rutnagherry (106) and Dharwar (16) are absolute and perfect, or whether, on the contrary, there are many cases in which the after effects (noticed by old writers and recent authorities) disturb or delay the recovery of health.

There is a well authenticated case, in which the patient, bitten by a foorsa, recovered from the immediate effects, but his health was in some way permanently injured. He wasted and died after an interval of more than twelve months.

The whole subject is to be regarded as a series of improbabilities, of things difficult to believe or realise. Much divergence of opinion exists even among officers of great experience. Underlying all this is the terrible truth that many thousand persons are killed every year by poisonous snakes in India.

Any one who has any experience in examining evidence, or who understands what constitutes judicial proof, will admit there must be found in the returns at all events an approximation to the truth.

Otherwise they must assume that all the

Indian officials, past and present, who at any time have had any share in preparing or revising these returns, have all been smitten with judicial blindness, and laboured under the most extravagant and astounding delusions.

If, like Dogberry, they choose to affirm that the compilers of the returns "have committed false report," and "verified unjust things," and "to conclude, all lying knaves," they are on the horns of a dilemma as ugly as the horns of thc Zulu army—either they hold the faith according to St. Dogberry, or they admit the mortality.

Not 22,000—no hard and fast line, but an approximation (erring, probably, as stated elsewherc, on the score of deficiency) not exaggeration—there is no room for palliation. The returns are either unmistakably, deliberatcly, and intentionally false, or else, allowing a very broad margin for oversights and inaccuracics of every sort, over 20,000 pcrsons die from snakebite annually.

This may fairly be called a broad margin, for it means four times the mortality of the whole of the Western Presidency in the year 1856, or within a fraction of seven times the mortality of 1858.

It is not to be wondered at that the British public, hitherto in profound ignorance of the whole matter, refuses to give *tout d'un coup* its sympathy or belief or recognise so improbable a statement as to this great mortality from snakes in India; and it seems reasonable enough that there should be distrust and unwillingness to accept these big figures *en bloc*.

It would certainly tend to remove much of this darkness which hangs over the whole question if the Government would publish in the newspapers in the beginning of each year, in addition to the report of the mortality, some further particulars, among other items, two years of highest and two of lowest mortality, with some explanations as to causes, such as "offers of rewards stopped by order," "operations suspended during famine," &c., also report of recoveries and successful treatment.

CHAPTER IX.

AN illustrious writer in the "Contemporary Review," August 1878, said that "We do not care for the people of India. . . . Do we even care enough to know about their daily lives of lingering death from causes which we could so well remove. . . . Have we no voices for these voiceless millions."

With infinite respect for the writer and her opinions, we beg to offer some modification. The vast majority of the people of England know absolutely nothing about the people of India, and, therefore, do not care, as they do not care about the people of any other country of which they know *nothing*.

Secondly, there are many persons who know *something,* have been in India themselves, and dislike both the country and the people; who have suffered in health, lost relatives, and lived chiefly at the presidencies. The men of the presidency, lawyers or others, loathing the climate and seeing many of the worst specimens of the people, look forward to the time when they may quit the country, and then retain their dislike.

Thirdly, there are others, chiefly men of the services, who have had the better fortune to be thrown much with the people up country. They tell a very different tale of men who do not lie or cheat, and of excellent courage, as represented by Rajpoots or wild tribes, Bheel, Kolie, Bender, Goorkah, and many others. This, though it is not easy to define or explain, constitutes another element, viewing India and the natives under different conditions.

Administrators of districts who are far away in the jungles felt, and with reason, the most perfect confidence and security—who, in a word, though they have returned to England, still have a great yearning for India, the official labour, the hunting, and the people.

Soldiers also, particularly those who have

had the good fortune to serve with irregulars who have met many men the fac-simile of the old pensioned Russaldar in "the City of Sunshine," and can tell of others who have distinguished themselves in action, and otherwise behaved well in the various risks of jungle sport, and others who have proved loyal and faithful under desperate temptations, like the Child of the Mist in the Dungeon ("Legend of Montrose").

The regard is reciprocal—gratitude and devotion without measure. It may be asserted that, when an officer has acquired a native's full regard, the native will not hesitate to risk his life. In action with insurgent Bheels in the Nasic Hills (1857–8), a sepoy noticed a rebel taking a deliberate shot at his officer, whose attention was directed elsewhere. The sepoy put himself in front, and was shot instead.

What precautionary measures ought to be taken in attempting to found a colony in a jungle district would require a detail beyond present limits, but some sort of warning may be gained from past failures.

There are different degrees of unhealthiness in a jungle district. A tract shut in among hills, where there is no water except from small streams or nullahs, offers a climate which even Bheels cannot support; and higher ground in the vicinity of such a valley is as bad.

But there are large tracts deserted since Ameer Khan and other ruffian leaders of Pindarees ravaged Khandeish. These can be redeemed, old wells can be dug out and repaired, the jungle grown up can be cut down, and the country brought under cultivation.

Moreover, it is perfectly well known that clearing a jungle does not at once restore its normal condition of health to a district. There intervenes a period of particular unhealthiness. This is said to be the case not only in India, but in other countries.

But the risk is small to Bheels, &c. They can support a climate which is death to others; though it is proved, as before stated, *there are localities in which Bheels suffer severely*, as shown by the condition of outposts unavoidably maintained among the hills during the mutinies.

This much may be said to meet the objections sure to be raised—that many attempts to colonise jungle districts have failed, but it is not expedient to try the experiment in localities notoriously and necessarily malarious. There are others which have been under cultivation and have been abandoned, not on account of the climate, but from fear of the Pindaries. Khandeish was partly depopulated and has not recovered, and the introduction of snake-killing colonists would be beneficial in that way also.

But it is not Khandeish alone, but there are tracts of country stretching down to the south where Hullial-Sambrani has a proverbially bad repute for extreme unhealthiness.

It might be satisfactory to give an instance of a jungle district redeemed, not far from Hallial, just referred to. There is another a few miles to the north, called the Kakerie Keriat, which was kept as thick jungle by the chief of Kitoor as a sheltering place for his bands of marauders. Some years after his death attempts were made to redeem this tract of fertile land, and it was done by villagers living somewhat beyond the line of malaria, who were induced by a judiciously low assessment to cultivate the land, and who went in the morning and returned to their own villages in the evening. In the course of a few years this Kakerie Keriat became as healthy as any other part of the district.

It is very important that the proposed snake-killing colonies should not fail. Some of the conditions which form part of what may reasonably be expected to constitute success are:—That the land at no distant period—say the time of Ameer Khan—was under cultivation; that means be taken to restore old wells, or to make new; and that the villagers should not depend for their water supply on the nullahs. The settlers must be *bonâ fide* Bheels, or Kolies, or Benders, Karawa, or Wudder, according to the district. The Momlutdar, or native chief of the district, should be a Mahomedan or Parsee.

Starting with the *sine quâ non* that the snakes must be killed, the *modus operandi* must be left to the officer and his subordinates charged with the duty; there should be no demonstration, the work should be carried on as quietly as possible, and, in cases where necessary, the head of the reptile ought to suffice as evidence and the rest be disposed of.

There is a class in all the prisons throughout the presidency who are deservedly pitied by officers in charge of prisons and medical officers as the class before referred to—Bheels, Kolies, &c.—because they suffer so much from confinement*; these men should be employed in killing snakes—a congenial employment, in which they would do good service with small reward.

It is of course understood there would be no compulsion—none would be needed. Some small indulgence and a remission of the term of their sentence, these would suffice. These men are now sent out some distance from the prisons to make bricks, burn lime, or charcoal —let them kill snakes.

How far the assistance of the district police may be utilised, and what agency in connection with them may be made useful, under what circumstances rewards ought to be offered, and how far paid agents are to be preferred—these also, and many other points which one might be tempted to refer to, are all obviously more fitly left to the officers now in charge of the districts, for any knowledge or experience of a bygone day will only help as a guide to certain great principles which cannot alter the one now under consideration—that upwards of 20,000 persons should not die of snake-bite.

* And also for their manly characteristics, courage, and truthfulness.

We may with truth aver that real attachment and mutual respect may and do exist between the European officer and the native, and those who like the natives least know them least.

Sir Philip Sydney said that "Chevy Chase," though sung by "an old blind crowder," moved his heart more than a trumpet. The blood tingles in the veins of the stout men of Cornwall when they hear another old ballad about Trelawney—

> And must Trelawney die?
> And must Trelawney die?
> Then twenty thousand Cornishmen will ask the reason why.

If now, in ending, one may venture to borrow something of the spirit of the old song, and say—

> Must all these thousands die?
> Must twenty thousand die?
> Let Scot, and Celt, and Englishman now ask the reason why.

CHAPTER X.

PENDING the issue of a brevet, in which a distinguished Peninsula colonel, fearing to find himself excluded on the ground of his religious opinions (Roman Catholic), informed the Horse Guards that he was "of the religion of which they made *general officers*."

Whenever there is an increase of mortality in a district, there is want of energy on the part of the district officers and the police. If the religious opinions of a district officer are in conflict with his duty, he should be found employment elsewhere, and some one appointed who is of the religion of which the Government makes "*district officers*."

In case it should be supposed that Brahmins

are included in this category, it may be distinctly said they are not. The Brahmins, who served formerly in the southern Mahratta country, were, as a rule, a most intelligent class of men, who, though they themselves did nothing contrary to their caste rules, would not have prevented others carrying out the orders of Government.* His caste opinions never prevented a Brahmin native officer doing his duty well. Superior in intelligence, and equal in courage, he was always valuable.

Some suggestions are offered in parts of the text, of which the following is an abstract:—

Wudders and others, who are, or may be made, efficient agents in the destruction of snakes, to be induced to colonise by grants of rent-free land.

Prisoners (volunteers) selected from the wilder tribes, who suffer most from imprisonment, to be sent out in parties to kill snakes, as they are now sent out to make bricks, burn charcoal, &c.

The neighbourhood of villages to be kept clear of harbouring-places for snakes. Old

* The observation is limited to Mahratta and Canarese Brahmins. Of others we have no personal experience.

walls and rubbish should be cleared away. Sometimes a patch of waste ground with coarse grass, weeds, or bushes, will be found infested with snakes.

The villagers should be persuaded to put coarse gravel around their houses; it is generally believed that snakes, as a rule, will not cross over coarse gravel.

All municipalities should be compelled to do their duty, after the example of Bangalore.

An extension of Rugtamania recommended.

For the protection of harmless snakes, *rough drawings or paintings of the six or seven poisonous snakes* of the district to be put up in every school and Amils kutcherry.*

Though certain kinds of gas, which destroy every other form of animal life, have been tried and failed with snakes, it does not necessarily follow that some other may not be found.

The essential oil of tobacco is said to instantly destroy the puff adder in South Africa.

There are many places where snakes congregate in vast numbers in India as they do in parts of America. A wholesale destruction by fire or gunpowder *en masse* appears to be the

---

* No reward to be paid for any other. No disappointment or breach of faith could be felt or alleged.

better and more effective plan, instead of attacking single snakes.

The foorsa (*Echis carinata*) is said to be found in great numbers on the hill fort at Rutnagherry; probably also in some of the other forts and islands of the Concan.

At Jingiwara, half-way between Verumgaum and Anwarpoor on the Runn, a mound (probably old ruins) is said to swarm with cobras. Many other places might doubtless be pointed out where an immense number of reptiles, might at once be swept away if a fitting agent could be found.

It may be worth considering whether it is not possible to increase the number of birds and animals which prey on snakes. There were no crows at the Mauritius; the planters obtained from India the bird called "mina," which, being a carrion bird, offered little temptation except to persons bent on mischief, who were liable to a fine of five dollars for killing a mina. The bird, being thus protected, multiplied exceedingly and spread over the island, and answered the purpose for which it was introduced, viz. to destroy grubs and other insects which injured the sugar-canes.

Certain cranes are said to destroy snakes in

great numbers. Perhaps something might be done to increase their number and protect them, also the mongoose.

Nothing would tend more to popularise a well-ordered system of snake-killing as rughta-mania,* the meaning of which is *a small grant of rent-free land to the heirs of those who died in defence of the village boundaries.*

Now we suggest it should be extended to snake-killers in the Government service, to be given with certain restrictions in particular districts in which there exists strong, though covert opposition. By "well-ordered system" is meant the employment of an efficient agency acting under special orders, according to certain plans defined by authority; above all, without beat of drum, taking care not to give unnecessary offence by any display or parade of the work on which they are employed.

There is much more, but not of interest to the general reader. Before concluding, if any entertain doubts—which they may easily do, seeing the returns in conflict and broad divergence of opinion among

---

* Blood Iram.

authorities—let them read the report of the Calcutta Snake Commission. If such details do not interest, at any rate the letter of the President at the end deserves very particular attention.

The President has no doubt as to the magnitude of the evil or the possibility of reducing it. While recognising the returns as imperfect, he considers the defect is not in exaggerating the mortality.

Compare a man preaching before the University. The same in his own parish. *Altero.*

If asked to give a lecture about herpetology, we should, *quam cito,* "evacuate Flanders." In our parish (administration in India) we are, or used to be, on familiar ground, and fear no man. The old saying, "No case; blackguard the plaintiff's attorney," will not apply here. We *have a case,* and a very strong one, though so sad. It is action that is wanted, not lamentations or tears. The more the matter is examined, the better for India. *Et tant pis pour les serpens.*

John Bull has the case set before him in a form which he must understand: that is enough; *habet foenum in cornu.* "War Bull."

Our task is done. There is much more to

be said on the subject, but it must be said or written by a younger man, with more recent experience. *Valde et valete.*

DESTRUCTION OF LIFE BY HYDROPHOBIA.

OWNERLESS dogs are allowed to stray about in the towns and villages of India in great numbers, and occasion an annual loss of life from hydrophobia. This, though a very serious, is distinctly proved to be a preventible evil, requiring only resolute and unremitting action on the part of certain agents charged with the duty, which should, and can be, done without parade or offending any one's prejudices or feelings.

The Government Records will show how much the subject has engaged the attention of the authorities in Western India during the last thirty years.

There was great alarm in England two years ago; the police had special instructions, and the dog-tax was increased one-third. We are not able to give the exact amount of mortality in all England, but the deaths from hydrophobia are supposed to have been about forty. In the districts of the Bombay Presidency in 1856–58 the mortality amounted to—

In 1856 . . .	105*
1857 . . .	46
1858 . . .	61

In 1858, 53,239 dogs were killed.

The records for 1859 ought to show a great reduction in the mortality, but we cannot supply that information.

Later returns show that there is still a high mortality in India from hydrophobia, and any one with any experience of the country will not hesitate to declare that *efficient measures are not taken to keep down the numbers of stray dogs.*

Recognise the principle that no man of any condition or caste has any right of ownership in a dog allowed to stray about a village, that such dog is a public nuisance and a danger to everyone, and ought to be removed.

But this has been often said before, and, better still, *acted upon;* then, after an interval

---

* A mortality of 105 in England would have created considerable excitement.

of time, vigilance relaxed and the work had to be done over again.

It is so important, the attention of the reader is particularly directed to what Dr. Morehead reported, *vide* page 95.

The present mortality from hydrophobia is much in excess of what it ought to be, with ordinary measures, as already indicated, vigorously carried out.

No doubt sometimes a case of hydrophobia occurs for which it is difficult to assign a cause, and a mad jackal appears and does much mischief: but these are exceptional cases.

The main cause of hydrophobia in India is the *ownerless dogs* which infest the towns and villages, lying about the streets in such numbers that it is, or was, not without danger a man passed along a street on foot. Take Cambay, for example, to pass from the Old Factory to the Bunder Gate, or the streets in Ahmedabad.

There appears to be no reason why licences should not be granted to keep dogs; it would strengthen the hands of the local authorities, help identification, and in the event of action for injury sustained, might be of material use to establish ownership.

The first object is to encourage those who like dogs and wish to keep them for sport, or any other reason, *to take care of them;* and the second, to be kept always and steadily in view, is that *every ownerless vulgo-pariah dog* is to be regarded as *hostis humani generis,* from his exposed and neglected condition very likely to become rabid, and therefore an extremely dangerous nuisance, to be removed as speedily and quietly as possible. Increase of hydrophobia means *undue and improper toleration of ownerless dogs, apathetic district officers, negligent and inefficient police.* It requires all three to increase the mortality from hydrophobia.

The following is the substance of a correspondence illustrating very clearly the difficulties the Government and their subordinate officers had to contend against in dealing with ownerless dogs and hydrophobia twenty years ago, published by order of Government on a petition, dated 20th January 1859, addressed by the inhabitants of Ahmedabad to the Right Honourable the Governor in Council of Bombay, relative to the destruction of dogs in the city of Ahmedabad :—

"Most humbly showeth,—That your petitioners most humbly beg to present the following few lines to your Lordship's humane consideration regarding the indiscriminate destruction of the dogs of this city, recently ordered by the police authorities, which circumstances have been a cause of deep regret to your petitioners and all their co-religionists.

"That necessary arrangements are always being adopted at the expense of your petitioners and mahajuns at large to remove such dogs as are *reported to be rabid*,* or giving any kind of nuisance to the people; and in consequence of your petitioners' former representations, Government were pleased more than once to issue orders to prohibit the indiscriminate destruction of these animals, and for some time past the practice of killing dogs was put a stop to, to the great satisfaction of the people.

"That on hearing the wording of the recent royal proclamation of Her Most Gracious Majesty the Queen, assuring the people that Government officials will not be permitted to interfere in any matter connected with the religion of the natives, and that the prevailing

* Who reported, and to whom? And who removed the dogs reported to be rabid?

customs and usages of this country will be duly respected, your petitioners were humbly induced to trust they should never have occasion again to complain about such matters as the indiscriminate and wholesale destruction of the poor harmless animals like dogs. And it is, therefore, with the greatest reluctance that they are again obliged to trouble your Lordship on the subject.

"Under all the circumstances of the case, your petitioners are respectfully induced to trust that your Lordship in Council will graciously be pleased to prohibit the indiscriminate destruction of dogs, and will thus put a stop to a great uneasiness and mortification to which all the Hindoo inhabitants of this city are subjected.

"And for this act of mercy and consideration towards the feelings of your petitioners, they, as in duty bound, shall ever pray."

Government having referred the petition to the Commissioner of Police, he made the following report on it:—

"The Commissioner of Police has the honour to report, for the information of Government, that the facts are not correctly stated in this petition.

"No measures of any kind have been ordered or steps taken at Ahmedabad which have not been in force during the last four years; the statement to the contrary in this petition is without any foundation whatever.

"It might be inferred that the local officers had been over-zealous, and that sufficient tact and precaution had not been exercised to avoid giving unnecessary offence.

"The Commissioner is well aware that the very contrary is the case; he received complaints yesterday as to the extent of the existing nuisance, and such complaints are only too well confirmed by the hydrophobia mortality returns, which show that Ahmedabad has more casualties than any district in this Presidency save Ahmednuggur.

"It is sufficiently evident that, *if the dogs were removed as stated by the petitioners, they could not be killed by the police.*

"Any one who chooses to keep a dog within house or enclosure may do so without interference, but no one has a right to convert the highway into a dog-kennel, or turn the streets into harbouring-places for dozens of stray dogs to the extreme danger of life of Her Majesty's subjects.

"It is somewhat remarkable that the petitioners at Ahmedabad cannot understand the proelamation as well as the people of Surat, Poona, and other cities and towns, the latter comprehend fully that the proelamation sanctions no act under prctext of religion on the part of any seetion of the community, which act, whcther of omission or commission, endangers the life or property of the rest of the community.

"The pctitioners are well aware that it was not till after years of unavailing remonstranee, every effort on the part of the local offieers, and report from the Judieial Commissioner, Mr. Frere, that the Governmcnt took any steps in the mattcr.

"Do the petitioners pretend to any right of ownership? If so, why don't they exercisc it, have kennels as they have stables, like European offieers and native ehiefs, many of whom are fond of dogs, and prove it by taking care of the animals, give them shelter as well as food, and do not allow thcm to run about in the streets, lay out in the sun, and go mad, involving death to some and a frightful peril to the whole community.

"The idea of the Banians in Gujerat as to

what constitutes toleration are very remarkable.

"The Banian avoid hardship, exposure, war, occupies himself with trade, usury, &c. leads a sedentary life, and consumes no animal food. The European and all the war-like classes, Rajpoots, Seiks, Mussulmans, Maratha Kolees, require and consume animal food.

"The Banian is not content that he is neither required to eat, nor catch, nor destroy any creature having life, but he must needs attempt, and (when he dare) will use force and intimidation, to prevent the Mussalman, Maratha Kolee, &c. from catching fish or procuring sheep from those who will sell.

"The fact is notorious to all who are acquainted with Katiwar and Ahmedabad, the Banians have been known to break the fishermen's nets at Gogo, prevent Mussalmans killing sheep at Dholera, quarrel about fishing in the river at Ahmedabad as in the sea at Gogo, and, from a report received yesterday, have attempted to prevent poor people catching fish in the public tanks at Veerumgaum, with all which thcy have no more right to interfere than with the worship in a Mussalman mosque.

"The Commissioner of Policc begs to suggest

that the petitioners be informed, once and for all, that the first care of Government is for human life, the security of which is not compatible with the toleration of the nuisance of stray dogs; that stray dogs will not be allowed in any road, street, path, or bye-way at Ahmedabad, or anywhere else.

"Instead of standing forward as advocates and supporters of a dangerous nuisance, and the champions of animals *which are not their property*, the petitioners would better shew their appreciation of Her Majesty's proclamation by extending to others the toleration they receive themselves, and by studiously abstaining from interference with the habits and necessities of life of other classes of the community."

The Government dircted that orders should be issued accordingly.

One hundred and five deaths from hydrophobia are reported by the magistrates to have occurred in this presidency, as stated below, in the past year:—

Ahmednugger	23
Poonah	13
Suttara	13
Dharwar	9

Rutnagherry	9
Ahmedabad	7*
Khandesh	7
Taunah	6
Surat	5
Belgaum	5
Sholapoor	4
Kaira	4
Total .	105

Several thousand ownerless dogs have been destroyed; in the cities and towns where stray dogs formerly swarmed, a great diminution is perceptible. Every effort will be continued to lessen the risk to all classes of the people from deaths by hydrophobia.

The prejudices of a certain class are opposed to the destruction of animal life under any circumstances, but the mass of the native community appreciate the measure and understand that the sole object in view is to secure them from the risk of a horrible death.

The extent to which human life has been

* This was an exceptionally good year. The mortality had been within a fraction as high as Ahmednugger, and has risen since.

sacrificed from the cause specified is not fully shown by the returns. Some of the magistrates are decidedly of opinion that considerable allowance must be made for unrecorded deaths from hydrophobia,—this also applies to the recorded deaths from snake-bites. Greater accuracy may be relied on, with, it is to be hoped, a marked decrease of mortality, in the returns which will be submitted hereafter.*

As regards hydrophobia, on the authority of the medical transactions, it will be found that in the presidency hospitals *only two cases came under Dr. Morehead's observation in the course of ten years, from* 1838-48.

Subsequently, *four* cases having occurred in one year, Dr. Morehead observed that "*this very startling increase of this fearful evil led to the inference that preventive measures had been relaxed.*" The mortality in the districts of this presidency in 1856 was 105.

Shortly before he resigned the service, Dr. Gibson, Conservator of Forests, reported to the Government of Bombay that he had discovered

---

* The Report of 1859 ends here.

a remedy for hydrophobia,—whether prophylactic or a cure for developed hydrophobia is not clear; but designated *preventive,* it most probably implies that it was to be used as a prophylactic to eradicate or prevent the development of the virus.

Dr. Gibson, as Conservator of Forests, travelled much and had great opportunities for the prosecution of his botanical and geological researches. Though somewhat eccentric, he was much respected and trusted by the natives —one they would be likely to confide a secret to—in this case notonia as a remedy or preventive of hydrophobia. It is only surmise so far. The natives knew of the existence of the plant, and ascribed to it certain properties (about which English botanists knew nothing), which Dr. Gibson would certainly have tested and proved to his own conviction before he made any report to Government.

As almost every conceivable remedy has at one time or another been tried (*vide* list in Appendix, copied from the "Daily Telegraph"), notonia was not considered with much confidence—in fact, so little was previously known about it, that in some botanical work it appears as "a mild laxative," and not likely to be of any use in hydrophobia. The Assistant Collector in charge of Jooneer, who, like everyone else, had a high opinion of Dr. Gibson's ability, evidently believed he had good grounds for the conclusion he had arrived at, and reported to Government accordingly. Consequent on this, experiments were made at the Poonah Hospital, but they were not considered conclusive or satisfactory. Nothing decisive appears to have been done.

Through Messrs. Corbyn, of Bond Street, Mr. E. Kent, recently from Bombay, has supplied some very important information, as follows:—

Notonia corymbosa is a herb which grows to about twelve inches; the inflorescence is a corymb with blue petals.

The plant is found wild in the plains of the Deccan and is considered highly poisonous by the natives. It does not grow in the north-west of India, and inquiry elicited that it was not to be found in the Horticultural Gardens at Poonah. *Notonia grandiflora* of which *Notonia corymbosa* is only a many-flowered variety, inhabits dry, rocky localities in the Madras Peninsula. It was brought forward in 1860 by Dr. Gibson as a preventive of hydrophobia —an infusion—also pills to be taken three successive days. Formerly considered by botanists as a mild laxative, it appears in Bentley's Manual of Botany (1870) in its (we hope) true character, as a preventive to hydrophobia.

There are instances in which persons bitten by rabid animals have been treated with notonia obtained from Dr. Gibson and been saved —(D. L.) one a case of mad jackal—another recently, a lady at Bombay bitten by a mad dog (E. K.).

Considering the great importance of the question, it appears to warrant further inquiry. Unless it has been tried and found worthless, it is difficult to account for the herb not appearing in the Poonah Horticultural Gardens.

Any one who knew Dr. Gibson would incline to the opinion of the Assistant Collector before referred to. He was much too wary to put forward a theory without good evidence in its support.

If three medical men were called upon to consider and report on all the facts—cases treated in hospitals or elsewhere—supposing it is not a success in cases of hydrophobia developed,—Is it preventive? Has it, used as a prophylax in any cases of assumed rabies, prevented the attack?

It seems to be the opinion of the best authorities that cautery, actual or potential, is the best safeguard against the virus of the dog in a rabid state, and there is hardly any conceivable case in which it could not be administered. But no adjunct is to be rejected if it will save the small per-centage of cases which are said to occur, in which hydrophobia is developed notwithstanding the cautery.

Hydrophobia has before now appeared among fox-hounds: despairing of a remedy, the whole kennel has been destroyed. This is a case in which, if notonia were a recognised efficient remedy, much valuable property might be saved. The hounds suspected to have been bitten, would be isolated and treated with notonia.

There is very little to be said about the destruction of life by wild animals in Western India, simply because it is comparatively insignificant.

As mentioned elsewhere,—ten years ago there were so few tigers in Khandesh, officers used to go from Khandesh to Central India for tigers: the swarms which existed in Captain Outram's time had, under his and others' combined exertions, disappeared; occasionally a man-eater was reported in the north or south Concan, or some other district, who did considerable mischief.

It may be accepted as a rule that most frequently a man-eating tiger has several haunts and wanders over much ground. The party attacking should be sufficiently strong to admit of division, so that all the known resorts of the beast should be visited simultaneously.

As a rule, bears and bisons never molested anyone without provocation. Wolves were heard of in the eastern districts. But the mischief occasioned by wild beasts was, compared with the other preventible causes, insignificant; the records show this was not the case in the other presidencies.

Many lives were lost formerly from persons falling into unfenced wells, or wells of which the fence had been allowed to fall into disrepair. The subject was fully considered under Lord Elphinstone's Government, and orders were issued which were calculated to abate the evil. Nothing further need be added on this point, except the expression of a hope that these orders are still rigidly enforced.

APPENDICES.

PART I.

THE following is reprinted in Allen's *Over-Bombay Gazette,* and is well worthy of some much

STATEMENT.

"*Snakes in the South Konkan.*—An interesting letter on snake-bites is published in the *Asian,* from which we extract the following:—'Of all the snaky places, with the *doubtful** exception of Sind, in the Bombay Presidency, the Ratnagiri, or south Konkan district, is the snakiest, and of all the snakes found therein, the *phursa* or *Echis carinata,*† is by far the most common. With a population of just over a million, the deaths from snake-bite have for years past averaged considerably over a hundred.‡ A few deaths are caused by cobras§ and dabois,|| but in the great majority of cases the fatal instrument is *Echis carinata.* In 1856, of the 153,090 venomous snakes for which rewards were given in the Bombay

APPENDIX A.

---

land Mail, from a correspondent of the notice, as containing information on disputed points.

Remarks.

*" *With the* doubtful *exception of Sind." Why doubtful? The returns from Hyderabad show the mortality there is, and has been for some time, much higher even than Rutnagherry at its worst time.*

† *The writer truly states that, of all the snakes found in Rutnagherry, by far the most common is the* Echis carinata.

‡ " *For years past the deaths from snake-bites have averaged considerably over a hundred." " The writer, whose letter is so important and valuable, has on this point been misinformed. The deaths, which in* 1856 *had been about* 250, *have never amounted to* 100 *except in* 1875, *when they rose to* 144. *More recently the number has been reduced to* 30 (*vide p.* 60).

§ *The population of Rutnagherry was* 665,238 *in* 1856; *if it is over a million now, it is a remarkable fact, unless more territory is included.*

Presidency, no less than 140,828 were destroyed in Ratnagiri, and of these upwards of 90 per cent. were phursas. In 1872, at a reward of two annas a snake, 115,921 snakes were killed in eight days (Dec. 2–10). The configuration of the country, consisting of low rugged hills and rocky plateaus, is especially favourable to this species. Near the coast the uplands are thickly covered with loose laterite boulders, while further inland, at the foot of the western Ghâts, the laterite is replaced by trap. Under these rocks and boulders the phursas make their habitation and multiply exceedingly. They are seldom seen by day, not leaving their hiding-places, as a rule, till darkness sets in, and then woe to the shoeless traveller who steps unawares on one.¶ The bite of the *Echis* appears to be fatal in about 20 per cent. of the cases. The action of the poison is comparatively slow.** The average of sixty-two fatal cases treated at the Civil Hospital†† gives death in four and a half days, though in some instances patients lingered up to twenty days.' "—*Bombay Gazette.*

The returns of 1855 *and* 1856 *showed that at that time the mortality in Rutnagherry was within a fraction of half the whole of the twelve other districts and the Province of Sattarah. If it had continued at that rate, the mortality up to the present time would have been over* 6,000. *But the returns show that there has been no such mortality.*

|| *Notice another very important fact. "In* 1876, *in all the Presidency,* 153,090 *venomous snakes were killed; of these,* 148,828 *were destroyed in Rutnagherry, and of these* 90 *per cent. were foorsas." "In* 1872, 115,921 *snakes were killed in eight days* (*Dec.* 2—10) *for a reward of two annas a snake."*

¶ *True: but during the rains they are found everywhere in houses, under rugs and mats.*

** *If this is correct, there is now a much greater percentage of recoveries than the old records show, the best being* 1864 (*at Rutnagherry alone*), *recoveries* 106. *The slowness of the action of the poison is correctly noted, but the writer does not appear to be aware of the oozing of blood through the pores of the skin, as described by Dr. Morehead and others."*

†† *Sixty-two fatal cases treated at the Civil Hospital show that the danger was not in abeyance at the period referred to.*

APPENDIX B.

THE following is a brief abstract of a memorandum supplied by a learned Professor at Christiansund in Norway.

"There is in Norway only one kind of poisonous snake, *Vipera berus,* or according to Linnæus, *Vipera prestis.*

"Cases of people being bitten by vipers are not frequent.

"Cases have occurred (very seldom) of children who have died by bites of vipers, but the writer has never heard of the death of an adult.

"The common treatment is by ammonia and brandy; oil is not used; sucking the wound and actual cautery are known and practised, and ligatures are applied when practicable.

"The symptoms are lymphatic or phlebitic, inflammation beginning from the wound and extending,—nausea, debility, and other indisposition. It is recognised that the poison is more active in hot weather.

"The previous summer (1877) having been unusually hot and favourable for snakes, an unusual number of vipers were seen."

This disposes of the alleged existence in Norway of any viper of more dangerous character. The above description of the reptile and the treatment (with the exception of the use of oil) corresponds precisely with the accounts of Bell and other writers, regarding the English viper as found in the New Forest, the Wyre in Worcestershire, and elsewhere in England, and (according to Wallace's Geographical Distribution) from Portugal to Saghalien,—but not in India.

APPENDIX C.

No one insists on the precise accuracy of the returns—only that they are not "cooked" or falsified with intent to mislead. Discrepancies in returns are not confined to India. In a discussion about street accidents, in the House of Lords, Lord Beauchamp stated that in 1878 only 124 were killed, and in 1869, 182, showing a *decrease* in the later or more recent returns. But the Registrar-General showed that 2,151 were killed in London streets by vehicles during the last ten years, so that there is no decrease, as supposed by Lord Beauchamp, but on the contrary there is an increase, and the correct numbers are 232 in 1878, against 192 in 1869.

The discrepancy is important, and not easy

of explanation, but no one for a moment imputes *mala fides* to either party.

Why should it be imputed to those who prepare the snake returns?

APPENDIX D.

THE following will serve to illustrate the question from another point of view, which, however, is not supported by any evidence whatever. (Copied and abbreviated from an Indian paper.)

"We are not, however, sure that as much can be said in defence of the expenditure of public money for the destruction of snakes, while a good deal can certainly be urged against it. Not one European in a hundred knows a poisonous snake. But in reality only three species* of snakes dangerous to human life are to be met with in the Bombay Presidency, viz. the cobra, the chain viper (*Daboia*

* Dr. Leith established the existence of six varieties of poisonous snakes, not including sea-snakes, which are also venomous.

elegans), and a small black snake, *banded* with white, which is known to naturalists as *Bungarus arenatus*.*

There is another prettily marked little viper,† which is common enough, but, as it is hardly a foot in length, its bite is very rarely fatal. Of the three species mentioned above, the *Bungarus* is "very inoffensive" ‡ and not common, while the chain-viper is extremely lazy, and generally gives warning of its presence by hissing furiously when anyone approaches,§ so that accidents from these two species are probably rare. The cobra, on the other hand, is one of the commonest

---

* There is no snake so named. *Clotho arietans*, or puff-adder, is found in Africa. *Bungarus cœruleus* is Indian, and very poisonous. *Bungarus fasciatus*, or *Banded Bungarus*, is not found in Western India.

† This "little viper" is *Echis carinata*, the pest of Sind and the coast districts of Western India, which *destroys more lives than all the other snakes together*.—*Vide* Imlach, Morehead, &c. &c., and, more recently, Appendix A.

‡ *Bungarus cœruleus* is very poisonous—and is not uncommon—and cannot in any sense be considered as "very inoffensive."

§ The Daboia, or Russell's viper, or Tic Polonga, here called "chain-viper," is an aggressive and very formidable reptile and exceedingly poisonous. The deaths from *Bungarus cœruleus* and *Daboia elegans* form important items in tho returns, particularly the latter.

snakes in India, as it is one of the most fatal in the world. Dr. Nicholson, who was appointed in 1873 to superintend the distribution of the rewards in Bangalore estimates the cobra population of that region as 1,000 per square mile. This calculation, if correct, will perhaps serve equally for any station in the Deccan,* as, for instance, Poona,† where the cobra finds both board and lodging on easy terms, in the holes of the field-rats, and pro-

---

* Such calculation will not serve "equally" for the Deccan; between Bangalore and Khandesh intervene the southern Mahratta country, fourth highest in the list of mortality, and Sholapoor, the lowest or most favourable.

† "As, for instance, Poona, where the cobra finds both board and lodging on easy terms in the holes of the field-rats, and probably does man more service in a year than all the mischief it does him in a century."

This implies that the destruction of snakes has had some effect in increasing the number of rats.

On this we may note that the animal which has done so much mischief is not a field-rat, but a jerboa. The Government commenced killing snakes twenty-four years ago; the plague of rats dates from two years; one *sixth* of the number killed were in the Sholapoor district, where there have always been, as now, very few snakes; the other *five-sixths* have been killed in the districts south of the Bheoma, where, as the returns show, *there are many snakes*—the mortality is the fourth highest in the list. In the districts where the greatest number of snakes have been killed we hear nothing about rats.

bably does man more service in a year than all the mischief it does him in a century. Throughout Bombay itself the cobra swarms, especially on places like Malabar Hill and Cumballa Hill and Parel.* That the cobra is so rarely seen is only another proof of its extremely timid and wary disposition. But snakes, indeed, shun man far more than man shuns them. Their first impulse on hearing his dreaded footstep is to run,† and among Europeans who wear boots, the possibility of of being bitten is so small that there is probably no fate incidental to man which it is altogether less worth our while to consider.‡ Natives, walking noiselessly, with bare feet,§

* If snakes "swarm" in any part of Bombay Island, it is very remarkable that there were, on the authority of Dr. Morehead, only fourteen deaths in five years, whereas at Rutnagerry (population, say one hundred thousand more) we find the mortality at the same period was two hundred and fifty in *one* year.

† All snakes do not run away; doubtful as regards *Daboia*, certain as to *Echis carinata*, which does *not* run away.

‡ The question does not regard Europeans who wear boots, but whether several thousand natives who die annually from snake-bites ought to be left to their fate, or whether proper measures ought not to be taken to reduce the mortality.

§ Many die from bites in the hand and other parts.

are of course much more liable to accidents, yet the statistics we have already referred to give the total number of persons killed by venomous snakes during the year 1878 at 16,812, or less than 1 in 10,000 of the population.* And it is not unlikely that we should be nearer the truth, if we *cut down that number by half*;† not only because snake-bite has been, since the days of Hamlet's father, a most convenient explanation of doubtful deaths, but because in hundreds of cases, where the bite of the snake would not have sufficed to kill the man, native methods of cure would complete the work, and put an end to his life."‡

---

* This has been emphatically denied elsewhere, and we again repeat that the theory is supported by no proof or evidence whatever.

† It is sensational, but false; such a conclusion can only be arrived at or warranted by *proving* that all the district officers throughout India are smitten by judicial blindness, and that all the Returns are "cooked."

‡ We have no reliable evidence on this point. The Hospital Records at Rutnagerry show a large percentage of recoveries.—*Vide* Appendix A., Note **.

APPENDIX E.

DOUBTFUL SNAKES.

THE poisonous snakes mentioned, were identified by the late Dr. Leith, but it is not to be inferred that he had decided there were none others existing in Western India; these above mentioned were (twenty-four years ago) rightly considered as constituting the element of danger which the authorities had to deal with.

Bungarus Fasciatus or other Bungarus or Bungaroid, though very eommon in Bengal, does not exist in the West, save only *Bungarus Cœruleus*.

Elaps ophiophagus was not mentioned by Dr. Leith, but there is a doubt about this formidable reptile — whether it is found in Western India, or not.

The natives generally believe in the existence of a small snake* which, from the sensation of burning its poison produces, is called "Ague Serpa." They attribute to this reptile the power of springing or jumping to attack.

A distinguished naturalist mentions the death of a snake-catcher in his employ, from the bite of a young Daboia, only a few days old.

Whether there is any *full-grown poisonous snake of diminutive size* in India, any reptile like Cuvier's *Vipera Brachyura*, appears to be doubtful.

Dr. Russell appears to have recognised its existence. He mentions three cases, one the house porter of the Governor Bourchier, who died instantaneously.

Two Sepoys of Captain Gowdie's battalion were bitten, and both died after some hours' interval with the same symptoms, *loss of sight and stupor, no convulsions.*

The snake described was scarcely six inches in length, of a dark straw colour, about the size of a large goose-quill, a flat head, with two very small eyes, which shone like dia-

---

* It cannot be identified by that alone, as other snakes, and even the scorpion, produce great pain, as of burning.

monds, and behind each eye was a black streak about three-quarters of an inch long.

Its mode of progression was not like other snakes, it made jumps or springs twice its own length (like the Cerastes Bruce described at Cairo).

Mr. Bourchier, son of the Governor, informed Dr. Russell that in the course of twenty years he had only seen two of these small snakes, and that the Portuguese called it "Cobra de morte."

Dr Russell, page 43, says that the belief was general, but that he, after much search, had never found a specimen of this snake.

There can be no doubt the Boodroo Pam (Russell, Plate IX.) was a bad specimen. The large green viper which Cuvier described, quoting Lacepede, Fitzinger, and others, is a very formidable reptile, variously designated *Bothrops Viridis*, *Trimeresurus Viridis*, &c. &c., and also identified as Boodroo Pam. A specimen was brought in to Rutnagerry at least three times the size of Russell's snake, a much darker green, and a singularly large head, the form and size resembling the Craspedocephalus, which does not exist in India, but to which the green viper noted above is closely allied.

PART II.

APPENDIX F.

Whether notonia is a remedy for developed hydrophobia will probably soon be, if it is not now, determined. It would be deplorable if, after all we have been led to hope, it is not assigned authoritatively the position claimed for it as a prophylactic.

It is well known in India that certain jungles are dangerous, and the march of troops for ordinary reliefs is prohibited by Government during the fever seasons. The records of Mhow and Malligaum will show how many lives have been sacrificed by officers risking the journey; but a notable case may be mentioned which is susceptible of proof, showing the value of prophylactic treatment. The hospital record of Ootacamund, Neilgherry Hills, of (circa) 1839, will show that a detachment of invalid soldiers in charge of an assistant surgeon, who had lost their way in the jungle and passed the night at Kakari* (prohibited), were, on their arrival at Ootacamund, ordered into hospital by the senior medical officer, and there put through a course of treatment of which quinine formed part. *Not one of these soldiers had the fever;* but the assistant surgeon, who was a friend and guest of the senior medical officer, persisted in declining treatment. About the tenth day after the night passed in the jungle the assistant surgeon was attacked by the fever, and his life was saved with great difficulty at the time, but health was completely wrecked, and he died about two years later.

In this country, where the cause of a fever and the time of infection are often uncertain, it appears as if the value of any treatment in anticipation can hardly be defined; but in regard to hydrophobia, as with jungle-fever, in the one case the bite, in the other the day or night passed in the jungle, mark the period from which the poison in each case may incubate, and during which it may be destroyed by prophylactic treatment.

---

* Certain halting-places were so notoriously feverish that warnings were given to travellers particularly not to halt *at night.* Those nearest the base of the hills were the worst.

It may be stated that people very generally understand the value of cautery, and need no persuasion to get the caustic applied, and *then* notonia should be used and the prescribed number of doses taken.

It is not contemplated that cautery should in any case be dispensed with, but cases are supposed to have occurred (probably from the cautery not having searched the wound sufficiently) in which hydrophobia has supervened after cautery; but the popular notion is sound and good, that cautery is a cure for the bite of a mad dog.

What the exceptional cases amount to it is unnecessary to inquire; if notonia will meet them, it is not to be despised or neglected.

Moreover, it is stated that persons who have been cauterised and saved from hydrophobia, have at certain intervals experienced very disagreeable symptoms indicating some latent cause of disturbance; if notonia can prevent this it will speedily be recognised as an important curative agent, not to supersede cautery, but as an additional safeguard against hydrophobia, and will be fully appreciated by those who have ever seen a case of hydrophobia.

London: Prin.ed by W. H. Allen & Co., 13 Waterloo Place.